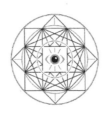

magic
and
miracles

21 Real Life Experiences from the Edges of Logic and Science

CREATED AND COMPILED BY

DR. ANDREA PENNINGTON

.

MAKE YOUR MARK GLOBAL

MAKE YOUR MARK GLOBAL PUBLISHING, LTD

USA & French Riviera

Magic & Miracles © 2018 Andrea Pennington, MD, C. Ac.

Published by Make Your Mark Global Publishing, LTD

Book cover design: Andrea Danon & Stefan Komljenović of Art Biro Network

Library of Congress Cataloging-in-Publication Data
Library of Congress Control Number: 2018913445
Magic & Miracles
Publisher: Make Your Mark Global, LTD
Fernley, Nevada
p.245
Paperback ISBN 978-0-9992579-8-2
Ebook ISBN 978-0-9994949-1-2
Subjects: Spirituality

Summary: In Magic & Miracles, Dr. Andrea Pennington presents 21 real life stories of people from various backgrounds and cultures who have found unseen forces supporting, guiding and healing them in their darkest hours. These stories cover events ranging from spontaneous experiences of divine love and recovering from childhood abuse, to personal struggles with identity and life purpose. What these stories all have in common is how they demonstrate that there are mystical forces and supernatural powers that can help us navigate the often troubled waters of life. There is great hope and inspiration to be found here.

Printed in the USA & UK

MAKE YOUR MARK GLOBAL PUBLISHING, LTD
USA & THE FRENCH RIVIERA

For information on bulk purchase orders of this book or to book Dr. Andrea or any of the authors in this book to speak at your event or on your program, call +33 06 12 74 77 09 or send an email to Andrea@MakeYourMarkGlobal.com

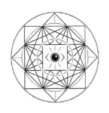

magic ,and miracles

CONTRIBUTING AUTHORS

Charlotte Banff - Stephan Conradi

Trude Dybendahl - Karin Eke - Halina Goldstein

Gitte Winter Graugaard - Diane L. Haworth

Malin Hedlund - Caroline Hoek - Elspeth Kerr

Paul Luftenegger - Andrea Pennington

Helene Philipsen - Ninet Sommer

Miriam Thiel-Alberts

Taz Thornton - Margaretha Tosi-Lesman

Lene Heiselberg Vang - Karena Virginia

Joyce Wazirali - Kimberly L. Wright

Preface

The book you hold in your hands is a unique blend of very mystical, true stories from some extraordinary authors. Each of them has opened up their heart to bring you insight into what led them out of pain, confusion and breakdowns into enriched lives full of beauty, joy and light. They will each help you open your mind and heart to your own world of magic and miracles.

Because our authors are from a variety of countries and we are publishing these stories in English you may notice that the spelling of words is a mix between in British and American English and that some phrases may be new for you. In light of the fact that many of our authors are not native English speakers, our team of editors has worked hard to make each story clear and full of the impact the author intended. It is our sincere hope that we have done their compelling stories justice and that you will be moved and inspired by them.

If you'd like to hear the authors in their own voice and watch as they provide context and color as to how magic and miracles have unfolded in their lives I invite you to visit www.MagicAndMiraclesBook.com to watch interviews conducted by the book's publisher, Dr. Andrea Pennington.

DEDICATION

This book is lovingly dedicated
to the beautiful souls of our world who feel lost,
unloved and confused

May this book help you reconnect
to the magical power within you

May you find peace and hope in your upcoming miracle

Contents

Introduction

Maybe you've always believed in magic and miracles, or perhaps you were attracted to this topic by a recent unexplained event. Whatever it was for you, I'm glad that you're here now. I've always felt certain that there is more to this world than we can see with our eyes or explain with science. That's not to say I'm not a big fan of the sciences because I truly am.

The practice of medicine was my first career before making a move into the television industry as the Medical Director and News Anchor for Discovery Health Channel in the US. You could definitely say that both careers were very 'sensible' and grounded in what skeptics may call 'the real world.'

It took my own miracle to encourage me to boldly share my spiritual side and, today, I proudly focus my energy on helping Lightworkers bring their messages and services to the world, with branding, mentoring, and publishing through my company, Make Your Mark Global. In this role, I am blessed to both witness and to hear first-hand accounts of everyday occurrences of miracles and magic.

I will tell you about my own miracle later on, but for now I'd love for you to sit back, relax, and hear from the wonderful Lightworkers who have co-authored this book with me. Magic and miracles are everywhere. I hope you find comfort and inspiration in these real-life examples.

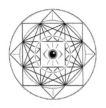

Part 1
Invisible Communication

When we are faced with painful life situations such as illness, loss of all kinds, financial strains or abandonment, it would be reasonable for us to hide, withdraw, or seek any form of relief from our pain. For our survival, it would even seem logical and wise that we should try to avoid adversity at all costs. When we feel that the pressure of the demands of life are beyond our own resources, we experience stress, fear and anxiety. These uncomfortable feelings usually signal danger; a potential death to the personality or to our physical self. But what if these are signals that we must look for unseen help, rather than give up or give in?

When we are weak, depleted or completely uncertain of our next step, we can call upon something greater than us — which may be our higher self, angels, guides, ancestors or saints — to fill us with additional knowledge support, help, love, strength or guidance. If we dare to do so — through prayer, meditation or total surrender to a Higher Power — we may just discover new wisdom downloaded into our mind or heart to solve these problems. We may find that a divine grace, an inner knowing or supernatural intervention will save us from danger, or turn 'poison into medicine.'

We are each endowed with more potential, strength and resilience than we often realize. Life's most painful lessons can be transformed into joyful blessings if we look to bring the best that is within us. We can do that by accessing the hidden resources that available to us, which each of the stories in Part 1 uncover.

Driven by Faith

Helene Philipsen

“I love you.”

That’s all his message said.

I looked down at the text on my cell phone.

“I love you.”

That was all. And somehow, I just knew.

Something was wrong. This day. Suddenly. Viscerally. Instantly. Without a doubt. I knew. Something was terribly wrong.

“Are you okay? Write me back. I’m worried now!” I texted back.

No response.

Similar to other casual messages I’d sent earlier in the day. No response.

“Hey handsome, answer me. Need a quick meet? You okay Dave?” Again, no response.

As I kept texting his work phone, the only phone he had, I felt a deep sense of panic spread through my chest, down into my stomach.

Looking back, this day began like any other with a completely normal morning in our home. It was business as usual.

We got up, chatted about the day ahead, ate breakfast with our boys and sent them off to school. I hugged and kissed Dave and watched him walk out the front door of the apartment.

It was my apartment, which he and his son had moved into just three months earlier. I still remember meeting them at the station. Standing there with one suitcase, each looking both hopeful and completely lost at the same time.

After my divorce a year prior I had only shared this big apartment with my son. But now it was the home of our new, emergent and blended family, where we could create the life we had dreamt of and always talked about. The same apartment that did not include his daughter.

This was devastating for Dave. His daughter had chosen to remain with his estranged wife, more than an hour away by train. A teenage daughter confused, unclear and still in the trap of her addict mother and there was nothing he could do about it.

Dave, had finally made it out. He was clear of the daily abuse. He was living in my home now. And we were evolving and growing and loving and working on life, this new life, together. It wasn't perfect. But it was ours. His. Mine. Ours.

It is easy to picture him as he made his way out of our new home to go to work that day.

Every workday, he maneuvered the same path. From our apartment, he'd take a quick left and down the street a few blocks to a cut-through path that runs behind the British Embassy. Then onto the pedestrian path that passes along the military cemetery, out towards the train station. I could imagine him as he wove his way through the peaceful, manicured cemetery plots out to the entrance of his workplace.

This path had become our place. It was our secret meeting place before we could be open about our budding friendship. A safe space to connect and see his smile and talk and get a break during our days, especially when the rest of the world felt like a hurricane of drama swirling around us. I would meet him there.

Maybe he was on our path now.

"I love you."

The text on my phone hadn't changed. And he wasn't responding. I had now switched to flat out calling. And calling. He wasn't answering his phone either.

Something was wrong. I could feel it through to the core of my soul.

It was after lunch, maybe two or three o'clock in the afternoon. I can remember the sunny blue skies of that day and still feel the tension rising in my chest even as the pit in my stomach grew deeper. I didn't process his message for long. Instead I quickly grabbed my keys and jumped in my car.

I drove without hesitation the few blocks to the entrance of our path. Without even parking the car, I slammed on the emergency brake and left it there. Panic swelling like a tide inside me, I ran down the path and into the cemetery shouting, "Dave! Dave!" No Dave. He wasn't there. Calling, texting. Constantly. Continually. "Where are you?!" No response.

Maybe he was out in front of his job site, taking a smoke break. This was my next logical guess.

I drove up and down the street several times. Back and forth. Still no Dave. And still no response. The white clouds blew frantically across the blue sky, dissolving, like a time-lapse video, and everything sped up.

Time was quickening in me as well. Like a clock was ticking down inside me.

"Where are you? Call me right now! I need to know that you are okay!" No response.

Who else could I call?

I had no other number than the one I couldn't stop dialing. I knew none of his colleagues. I had no one else to help. Heart pounding, legs shaking, left hand on constant auto dial and left hand barely holding the wheel. Where could I go? Where was he?

"Baby! Where are you!? Please call me!"

In a panicked trance, I drove up and down and back and forth between the path and our place and his job and around our neighborhood. Our beautiful Copenhagen neighborhood full of historic charm and unending waterfront that borders the brilliant blue Baltic Sea.

Desperate and out of ideas, I began repeating out loud to myself. To the universe. To something. To I didn't know what,

"Take me to him. Take me to him. Take me to him."

Like a manic mantra, I kept repeating it,

"Take me to him. Take me to him. Take me to him."

Time felt like it was passing fast. Slipping too quickly,

"Take me to him. Take me to him. Take me to him."

My right hand remained on the wheel. Just barely. All the while it methodically hit redial.

Then my right leg started shaking uncontrollably. I had to hold my knee down to keep my foot on the accelerator just to move the car forward while I continued to redial. I had no idea where I was going.

"Take me to him. Take me to him. Take me to him."

The car felt like it was driving itself. To where, I couldn't tell you. I couldn't track him. There was no find my iPhone app available. And he wouldn't answer.

"Take me to him. Take me to him. Take me to him."

My entire body was shaking now, but somehow I turned and drove down towards the water. Nowhere near where we would swim or even go for a walk, but down by Langelinie Pier. This was on the main Copenhagen harbor, not far from the iconic statue of Hans Christian Andersen's The Little Mermaid.

"Take me to him."

Seriously, where was I going? This was not somewhere we had ever visited together.

I turned onto the pier. The same pier, that in other seasons, brings throngs and masses of tourists as they pile off enormous cruise ships. Where they parade down gangplanks onto double decker tour busses to be taken around town. I passed a small ice cream kiosk at the top of dock, closed for the season.

Except for a silhouette near the kiosk, the pier was completely empty. I sped the car down toward the silhouette and slammed to a halt, mere steps from the water's edge. Two Danish fisherman looked up at me in shock. Not the catch they were considering this day. Hoping for some of the late season cod, they returned to casting their rods.

As I turned away from their tackle boxes and blue buckets, I thought I saw someone else, further down the dock.

I saw him.

I could see his frame. He sat slumped over at the edge of the pier. I could feel his weight. Barely stopping the car, I jumped out and left it running. My heart still racing as my mind scanned the scene.

Dave. My Dave. My darling Dave. Sitting. Still. His posture signaling defeat. His right hand in his lap. His left tucked up near his chest, holding something.

The smell of the sea filled my nostrils. Next to him, laid out with military precision were some of his prized possessions. Perfectly positioned and in immaculate order were his desert camouflage boots. His Navy issue desert camouflage backpack. A half-drained bottle of Jack Daniels. And several boxes plus the empty packaging of about fifty valium pills, which I could now see were what sat in his hand, held tight to his chest.

I saw it all. The scene. The goal. The text.

"I love you."

I yelled as I ran, "Dave!"

He turned. The disbelief evident. "How the fuck did you find me?"

I sat down beside him. For someone who doesn't drink, he didn't seem drunk or that affected by the pills, but I was uncertain how far into his plan he had proceeded. He was instantly emotional. Tears flowed freely as I moved closer and took him into my arms. Instinctively, I bumped his cupped hand of pills and we watched as they rained in an arc — plop, plop, plop — down into the sea. The water was so clear, we silently witnessed their descent.

I couldn't explain how I found him. It still doesn't make sense to me, even today. As I held him and let him cry, I suddenly heard myself say,

"Listen, if this is really what you want to do, then you are free to do it my love. It's your life and I love you and I forgive you. I will take care of your children like they are my own. If you want those pills back, I will find you more. This is your decision and no one else's."

He looked at me and listened.

But I also said to him, "If this is not what you want to do, and you want to go on living, then you will have to find a way to move through this, from this day. I can not live in fear of this ever happening again. Fear that the next time I'm two minutes too late. That the fishermen down there would find your body, bloated and blue. Or worse that you might never be found and I would never know. This is a decision that you have to make. Now. Just know that I can not live in fear that this will ever happen again."

He cried some more as we hugged. There on that pier. The cold water slowly flowing below our feet.

He finally asked me, "How do I know it will be ok?" And like that water, at that moment, I felt incredibly strong and incredibly clear. I looked at him and said "I don't know, but I know."

He took my hand and he said to me, "This will never happen again. I love you. And I will do whatever it takes to make sure it never gets this bad again." And without a shadow of a doubt, I believed him.

We put his things back into his backpack. I threw away the pill packages. I wanted to throw the bottle of Jack Daniels into the water, but he wouldn't allow me. He wanted to bring it home to never forget. Still, it sits in the back of a cabinet in our kitchen. Untouched. But there. A constant reminder.

We got back in the car. And drove the two kilometers home.

Not an hour after returning, Dave's son walked through the front door of our apartment. Home from school, a sweet boy, a lost soul just trying to navigate his 'new normal,' he had no idea what had transpired on this day. Dave looked at me and drew in a deep breath, slowing letting it go as he turned to his son and said, "Hey buddy, how was your day?" and gave him a hug.

We could both feel the physical turn of a page. This was a beginning. From that day forward.

The Aftermath

To be honest, it was traumatic for me, experiencing this miracle. The aftermath haunted me for the better part of a year. I would get flashbacks of my fear of showing up two minutes too late.

The journey I was taken on to find him, like a line straight from A to B, was nearly as testing. Something out of my control. Something I can't understand or even start to explain. It was inside me. It was outside me. It was me. It wasn't me. I am not a religious person per se. For Dave, that was God. For me…? I have no idea. It is difficult for my analytical brain to rationalize what went down that day. How did that happen? How did I find him?

What I do know is that he has made good on his promise for the last three and a half years. And on the days when I can see that he is not feeling good or seems low or just down, he can sense my stress. "Don't worry, I made you a promise." That promise? Quite powerful as it turns out.

The Dave I know is not a victim, but he has been one. He is responsible and accountable for his actions and what he will act on. That day, he was not the Dave that I knew. Or thought that I knew.

That was my first meeting with the demon that tormented him, the demon of depression. I thought I knew it. But I didn't.

I realized, that forDave, he felt that he had become a burden to us. He felt that his broken self was no one's problem but his and suicide seemed the solution. That this answer would set his loved ones free.

To me? That was mind blowing. It still is. Truly an illness, sneaky and powerful and something to be taken seriously.

During these three and a half years we have continued to grow. Together. Individually. And for sure as a family. We talk. A lot. And we take the traumas from our past seriously. We say the difficult stuff out loud when it pops up, even the real shameful feelings and memories. The work may be hard to do at times, but the benefits hugely outweigh the temporary discomfort of sharing. This is something I feel we have truly been rewarded for in life.

As I'm writing this today, it hasn't even been two months since we celebrated our love and our family in a beautiful marriage ceremony. Our three teens proudly walked the two of us up the aisle and stood by us as it all came full circle. Surrounded by people we dearly love, who know the essence of who we are to-day, I took in the delightful scent of pink and yellow flowers as we repeated our promise to each other.

"I will always love you, talk to you and share with you

— even when it isn't pretty."

About the Author

Helene Philipsen is a Life Transformation Specialist based in Copenhagen, Denmark. She works with women worldwide who are passionate about nourishing their body, mind and soul – but struggling to find the right path. Helene's expertise personally and professionally lies within life transformation, her core specialty being Freedom from Emotional Eating & Codependency. Her educational background is in Psychology and Recovery Coaching. She has committed her life to helping others because she wants you to know, that living lovingly and confidently – is possible for anyone.

Visit her online & connect on social media:
www.HelenePhilipsen.com
www.HelenePhilipsen.dk
www.facebook.com/helene.philipsen

A Miracle In the Wild

Taz Thornton

Miracles, huh? We tend to swat them away, don't we? Either that, or we assign them to cheesy Christmas movies or clichés about love at first sight.

But what if I told you that miracles are happening around us all the time, every day… that we've all probably benefited from them but haven't even noticed. Miracles don't have to be massive. They can manifest in the smallest ways or the tiniest of touches, as an unseen force, that make life feel easier.

Think about that time your train was delayed just long enough for you to leap aboard that day you were running late and really needed to make that appointment. Or that time you'd been thinking about someone all week, remembering how much you missed them, and then bumped into them in the supermarket. Think about the time you had a flat tire, then found out your delay meant you missed being in a multi-car pile up.

Yeah, we've all had them. We just didn't notice them or we've been conditioned to dismiss them as a coincidence.

Let me tell you, beautiful reader… I don't believe in coincidences. Sometimes, what happens in life is far too coincidental to be coincidences. This leads me into the story I want to share with you today. I want to take you back to a time when the 'miracles' I was experiencing through my relatively newfound spiritual path – or rediscovered for the first time in this current life journey – were too much for me to believe. It was a time when I needed proof. A time when I thought that this proof was clearly discernible in the physical world.

When I first started exploring shamanism with any real commitment, it felt as though all the pieces were finally beginning to fit together properly – it was as though I'd been trying to force all the jigsaw pieces together like a puzzle but I was not able to create a beautiful image. But when I surrendered to the path that had been calling me for so long, that's when I truly understood what 'flow' felt like.

If you're wondering what shamanism is, you'll find all kinds of conflicting ideas on Google. To keep things simple, shamanism is believed to be one of the oldest spiritual paths — certainly pre-dating religion. It's the belief that everything has an energy, that we're all connected, that the natural world around us is full of guides and teachers. As part of that path we 'journey' to the other realms, working with trusted spirit guides and mentors to bring back teachings, messages and healings for 'the tribe'. It's a beautiful path — one of walking in truth and beauty and absolutely taking responsibility for our own lives and actions.

Before I discovered the shamanic path, I was young and arrogant. Having spent years at the top of the corporate tree I had cynicism, self-doubt and a fair helping of ego drip-drip-dripping into my energy stream for years.

When I first realised there was a way to truly tap into that universal energy, that I could 'communicate' with all kinds of spiritual beings and elements of nature on a *soul* level, that we really were all connected, it blew me away.

It blew me away so much that, sometimes, I hardly dared believe it.

Every now and then, I'd hear how one of the other people sitting in my shamanic circle had been gifted with some kind of 'encounter' with one of the animal spirit guides they'd been working with; each time, it was filled with beautiful, power-full teachings and – if I'm really honest – each time I heard about it, it needled me, just a little bit.

You see, most of the guides I'd been connecting with in my shamanic work, and felt a deep connection to – my 'power animals', if you like – were no longer living on these British shores I call home. Most had lived here at some time or another, but had been hunted to extinction far before my time.

There were some I could connect with. I remember being delighted when the first animal I formed a real bond with in the shamanic journey was a muntjac deer; there was no way on earth I would have projected a muntjac deer.

Somewhere deep down, I knew that if I'd met with a wolf the first time I journeyed – one of the animals that had been invading my dreamtime since way before I was old enough to know what it was – I would never have trusted the experience to be true.

Fast forward to a few years after that. Animism and shamanism had become 'home' – they were in my blood now; it was as though they'd always been in my DNA, lying dormant until the exact circumstances all aligned for the magic to be awakened.

For me, shamanism wasn't something I dipped in and out of, or learned about in a workshop and then forgot about until the next time; shamanism and the medicine path were solidly and inextricably intertwined with me – a deep faith that informed my every move and filled the space between each breath.

By now, I'd built incredibly deep connections with the animal spirit guides I worked with most, as well as getting to know a few that had flitted in and out to deliver great teachings, or to set the wheels of some deeply important life lesson in motion.

One of those spirit guides was the hummingbird.

The first time my wife and I took a vacation to Canada (now one of our most favourite places), we spent time in Vancouver, Calgary and Banff. At the beginning of the holiday, we were having a conversation about hummingbirds and whether they were native to Canada. We honestly had no clue.

When we visited the Banff Park Museum, there were cases and cases of taxidermy specimens, but still I hadn't seen one alive and outside of a butterfly and wildlife park.

That's when I went into my old pattern of asking for proof. Surely, if my friends in England were getting these rich experiences with the physical representations of the spirit animals they were working with I could get something here in the Canadian Rockies, couldn't I?

That afternoon, my wife Asha and I ventured out onto an 'outback' horse trekking adventure. I love horse riding – always have. Asha was not keen on it, so we compromised and just settled for an hour-long trek.

Sometime in to the trail, taking in the beautiful surroundings and fresh, mountain air, there was a blur and then, right before my eyes, there was a hummingbird. It flew from left to right, hovering directly in front of my face for what felt like minutes but, in reality, was probably seconds. However long it lasted, the experience felt utterly magical to me – truly miraculous. I was on Cloud Nine and my inner star child was absolutely buzzing.

Gratitude. So much gratitude. I knew I shouldn't have asked for 'proof' (surely, I should have enough faith without that) but there it was. Proof. Literally, right in front of me.

A couple of days later the *real* miracle occurred. The one that, even now, feels as though it happened just beyond the shimmering, even though it was absolutely here and in the physical.

Asha and I had decided to take a walk to the Cave and Basin site in Banff. Just beyond there is a boardwalk leading up through the forest. Sure, there were signs warning of bears, but we'd seen plenty of other hikers and cyclists, so it must be safe enough, right?

As I walked through the trees, totally captivated by my surroundings – and still a little bit in awe of my hummingbird experience – I realised that Asha had gone off a little way ahead. That was okay. We were still on the boardwalk.

And then it happened.

Have you ever had that feeling that you're not alone? That *knowing* that someone – or something – is watching you, even though you don't or can't see another soul for miles? That was the feeling I had in that moment.

I stopped walking, dropped down in to my heart and tuned in as I had learned from my energy training. Something told me to look out across the lake – the stretch of water dividing the boardwalk I stood on from the other side of the forest. As I looked over the expanse of water, I slowed my breathing, and willed myself to relax and soften my focus.

There they were. Two yellow eyes, staring back at me through the trees. The creature moved forwards until it was completely unhidden by the foliage and stood, bold as brass, on the banks of the water across from me. A beautiful grey wolf – just like the one from the dreams I'd had since early childhood.

Our eyes connected and I felt a surge of energy in my heart, effervescently spreading through my body. It felt as though threads of the universe were winding between us both.

I continued to walk, and it walked alongside, the water between us feeling like inches as the power of our connection warmed me and seemed to bring us closer. I walked back the other way and Wolf turned with me, beautifully in step.

We repeated this kata[1] several times before suddenly, after Wolf had walked me all the way back the way I came, he stopped. I felt the connection begin to recede and felt a soul-deep *knowing* that it was time for us to leave.

By now, Asha was some way ahead of me, so I called out to her. She turned, looking confused as I beckoned her back towards me.

By the time Asha was standing next to me the wolf had disappeared back into the forest. I told her what had happened. As she was also by now following the same spiritual path she understood the importance of following the guidance I'd been given.

As we neared the exit, we saw park rangers filling the area and dashing out of their patrol cars. They hurriedly moved us on our way. It turned out they were there to evacuate the area. A mother grizzly and her young cub had been spotted wandering a little too

---

[1] Kata is a Japanese word for the detailed choreographed patterns of movements practiced either solo or in pairs.

close to civilisation, not far from where we'd been, and the area was no longer 'safe'.

Was this a coincidence? Well, you already know I don't believe in those.

Was it a lone wolf looking for lunch, whose intentions weren't as pure as I'm leading you to believe? It certainly didn't feel that way, so you'll just have to trust me on that one. Or not. The choice is yours.

Did I dream up the whole thing? No. That experience was a real as the words you're reading now or the sunrise this very morning.

Did that wolf save us? Was it a miracle? That's up to you.

I could have written about other experiences. I could have told you about the time we rediscovered, and bought, my mum's childhood teddy bear in a second-hand shop miles from home – recognisable by the unusual patch of darning on one paw.

I could have told you about the 'earth angel' who invited us to his table in a crowded restaurant and regaled us with wondrous tales of self-belief and wisdom before leaving us there, in awe and gratitude.

I could have told you about the car accident my wife and I shouldn't have survived – the one that directly replicated my wife's pre-cognitive vision – about how were speeding, head-on, into the path of an oncoming white van, our steering smashed and locked, until the wheels shifted at the very last second, only to immediately seize up again once we were on safe ground.

I could have told you the story of unwittingly walking around all day on a broken back, and living, largely without ill effects, to tell the tale.

I could have gone into the worlds of the fae and the supernatural and told you about the time a gnome ended up in my front room. But that tale — *that* one — would probably have been far too much for most people to comprehend.

My wolf story, though, that's the one that comes to mind when anyone asks me about miracles. Whatever you choose to believe, that's MY miracle. And, after all, miracles are always in the eye of the beholder.

About the Author

Taz Thornton is a motivational speaker who trained with the same team as Tony Robbins – so don't be surprised if she gets you firewalking! Her unique blend of 'tribal' communication tools learned from shamanic cultures, NLP skills, and years in top-line management means she can get right to the issues holding you back.

A TEDx speaker, bestselling author, visibility specialist, and award-winning empowerment coach, Taz gets people speaking honestly like you've never known.

Keep in touch:
www.TazThornton.com
Email: Taz@TazThornton.com

Find me across most popular social platforms.
#unleashyourawesome

The Power of the Mystical Law of the Universe

How a journey that started as a nightmare turned into a relaxed and untroubled holiday

Joyce Wazirali

In 2012 I was living and working in the Netherlands and I owned an apartment in Malaga, Spain. I bought this apartment as an investment and often rented it out. Out of the blue, I started having visions and an unsettling feeling that something terrible was happening in my apartment in Spain. It hadn't been rented in a few months.

I called my friend Laura, who would check my apartment for me. For a few months, I couldn't reach Laura and she didn't answer my calls or emails. I knew she was busy with her study of medicine and isolated herself from the rest of the world.

I put the feeling out of my mind but five months later, the uneasy feeling continued. Over and over again I was also having the same troubling visions about my apartment. I convinced myself that I was being irrational and tried to ignore them because I was afraid they might be true. The more I tried to ignore them, the stronger they became.

Since my early years, I get vivid visions, dreams and information about things happening. They all turn out to be true. And when they keep coming back, I know from experiences in the past that it's very serious.

Because my friend Laura didn't respond on my requests, I became worried and had to take action and go to Spain. Since there was no one else with a key of my apartment in Spain I was the only person to solve what I only saw in my visions. So I gathered all my courage and booked a plane ticket.

The morning of my trip my inner voice told me that it would be a journey with many ordeals. I didn't know when or where the ordeals would arise, or what they would be but I trusted my inner voice. My head said: *'it's all just fantasy. Don't worry.'* Whatever my head said, the feeling and visions kept on coming and became more clear. I was tense but had no other choice, I had to do what I had to do.

It was on a Friday. My airplane would depart at 4:30pm from Eindhoven Airport and I would arrive at 8pm in Spain. Shortly after that I'd be back in my apartment so I would have time to have a nice dinner in a restaurant in the village. That was my focus to suppress my intuition.

I checked in at the airport and was waiting for the boarding signs. A few minutes before boarding I heard an announcement about a plane that just crashed on the landing strip. Eindhoven is a small airport, and because of the crash all the flights were delayed for several hours. I thought: *this must be my first ordeal.*

The airport arranged buses to take the passengers waiting for the same flight to another airport. After waiting for a while, the buses arrived and I, along with the passengers on the same flight, got into four buses. We would drive to Maastricht Airport and then fly to Spain. All the while my unsettling feeling and visions were getting stronger.

The four buses were ready to depart when one bus driver discovered that his bus had a flat tire. I was happy that it was not the bus I was on until I heard another announcement. It was the rule to drive all four buses in a caravan. This meant all the buses had to wait until the tire was fixed. I thought: *this is my second ordeal.*

We finally arrived at Maastricht Airport. The next step was to get new airplane tickets from Maastricht Airport to Malaga. It was a springtime holiday and the airport was very busy with travelers. It was also busy with the airplanes departing and arriving so there was no airplane available for us. The airport had to order an extra plane to transport us to Malaga. No one knew how long it would take.

Because of the whole situation, I didn't think about having diner. I just stopped looking at the time and counting the ordeals. I knew there was something terrible waiting for me and I hoped it wasn't true.

When our plane arrived, we boarded immediately but the pilot had to wait until he got the sign to depart. Nobody knew how long it would take. An hour later our pilot got the permission to taxi down the runway and takeoff. I was happy to finally be on my way to Malaga, but I was also afraid of what I would find when I got to my apartment.

At 1:15am we arrived in Spain. I gathered my luggage and took a taxi to my apartment, which is on the first level of three floor building. The taxi dropped me off at 2:00am. I was tired, hungry, and thirsty but all the restaurants were closed. The street was also quiet because everyone was sleeping.

The moment of truth had finally arrived. As I stood in front of my building I was tense and worried as I slid my key in the lock of my door. When I opened it I saw a wet spot on the floor. My heart started beating wildly. I forced myself to step inside and when I did I shouted: '*Shit!*' which was exactly what I smelled inside my apartment and saw in my visions. Apparently, one of the two toilets in my apartment were backed up from my neighbors on the second and third floors and had dripped under the door into the living room and hallway of my apartment.

I had goosebumps all over my body. My greatest nightmare came true.

There I was hungry thirsty and tired, holding my luggage, with this overwhelming stench all around me. I looked in the kitchen cupboard for food and water. Unfortunately the cupboards were empty. The water from the tap had too much chalk in it and was not drinkable. It was late, my neighbors and friends were asleep and I didn't have a telephone number to call a taxi. Taking a walk to the village at 2:00am was not an option. It was very cold and the only way I could stay in the apartment was to sleep in the bedroom where the smell was not as overwhelming.

I went to the bedroom opened the window, put my coat on and covered myself with two blankets and tried to sleep. It was cold and I felt I was freezing. It was silent outside because everyone was sleeping. The only sound I heard was a cat in heat. In the bedroom the stench was still very bad so I kept my head under the blankets to filter it out but it didn't make a difference.

While I lay there hungry, thirsty, and cold, I felt like I was in the *avici* and the *gaki* world. These are the Japanese words for the *hell* and *hunger* world, the lowest levels in life as explained in Nichiren Buddhism. At that moment I thought of homeless people and beggars. I felt connected with them and realized what they are going through to survive. A feeling of compassion came over me and I didn't feel alone anymore. The feeling of hunger and thirst suddenly disappeared as well.

While I lay there miserable, captured in the *avici* and *gaki* world, I decided to pray for a solution to the problem in my apartment. As a Nichiren Buddhist, I believed in the power of chanting (praying) *Nam Myoho Renge Kyo* to the Universe for help. Which means *I surrender myself to the mystical Universal law of cause and effect* and *'turn this poison into medicine.'* The mystical Universal law is too complex to comprehend. From experience I know by chanting, situations change in a miraculous way.

That night felt like it would never end and my only hope was, to feel the warmth of the sun, get some fresh air, food, water and a much needed shower. Although the next day was Saturday, the problem had to be solved, but my Spanish was bad and I didn't know what to do. I heard my inner voice say that a solution would come, I just had to pray and put positive energy into my apartment.

At sunrise I sat and prayed to the Universe for help to break through this karma and *'to turn poison into medicine'* which means, *to turn the bad into good.* It was difficult to remain in the apartment because of the stench and cold, but I was convinced that change would come.

After I prayed I stepped outside to warm myself in the sun and went up hill to the village. The shops and restaurants in the centre were closed. I was the only person there. I settled myself on a bench in the sun. By the time everybody woke up, I started to call my Spanish friends including Laura for help but I was unable to reach anyone. Then I realized that using my brains in this situation wouldn't help. I had to follow my heart. I said to the Universe; *'I surrender!'*

A feeling of calm immediately came over me and I listened to the instructions from my inner voice. It was like an invisible hand was leading me to where I had to go, though I had no idea where. It was like the future was emerging *toward* me instead of me walking into the future.

The invisible hand led me back to my apartment. I opened the gate and followed the direction of my feet. I stopped on the pathway at my backyard. And I thought, *'what's next?'*

The invisible hand moved my head and I looked up to the balcony of my upstairs neighbor. There was a lady standing there. I said, "Hi, I'm Joyce, your neighbor from downstairs." She said:, "Nice to meet you Joyce. I'm Wendy. Can I help you with something?" When I told her what happened in my apartment, she was shocked and embarrassed. She told me about her neighbor upstairs from her. He was the president of our residential community and could help me. And he was a Spanish man.

I thanked her, then I went inside the building and knocked on his door. I was glad he was at home. When he opened the door I introduced myself. He held out his hand and said, "My name is Angel."

I thought, *'What a coincidence, after praying all night, a man named Angel could help me solve my problem.'* Angel lived with his lovely wife and two children.

When he heard what happened in my apartment he was apologetic and offered to help. He would do everything for me, but he needed to see the extent of the damage in my apartment before calling the insurance company. I gave him the key and was waiting while he went down to my apartment. After a few minutes Angel came back with a worried look on his face. He said that there was indeed a big problem.

Although the insurance company was closed on Saturday, Angel was able to reach the insurance employees on a their home number because he was the president of the community and had it in case of an emergency. Angel and his wife invited me to take a shower at their place and they gave me something to eat and to drink. I was not allowed to go back to my apartment until the insurance agent inspected it.

The insurance agent arrived and I gave her my apartment key. She went into my apartment and within a few seconds she ran out again and started to retch. Between breaths she said, 'don't worry, the problem will be solved, and your apartment will be cleaned up and disinfected.' She also suggested that I should stay in a hotel and the insurance company would pay the cost of the hotel room and also my plane ticket.

Angel arranged a five-star hotel at the beach for me and drove me there. It was like I was dreaming or watching a movie about someone else. I felt so much gratitude. And the burden I had been carrying was now gone. After settling down in my hotel room, I called my friends again and everyone picked up. I made plans to see them while I was in Spain and the rest of the week was a relaxed holiday with my friends. My neighbors, Wendy, Angel and his family and I became great friends.

My apartment was cleaned up and disinfected, the construction error in the building was solved and the insurance paid for everything.

A journey that started as a nightmare turned, within 24 hours, into a relaxed and untroubled holiday in a luxurious hotel on a private beach. That's the power of the Mystical Law of the Universe.

Lessons learned:

1. If you have a strong inner voice, listen to it.

2. Never give up.

3. If you believe in the power of the Mystical Law of the Universe, you will get the help you need or you will make a change for the better.

4. Believe in the invisible connections between people and that when we follow our heart, the people we need will appear in our life just at the right moment.

About the Author

Joyce Wazirali is an author and a holistic therapist for both individuals and businesses. Her company, Heliotropo, focuses on solving traumas that often prevents clients from realizing their full potential. She helps them gain strength now and equips them with the power to move forward.

Heliotropo came to be after 30 years of study and experience with people, business development and growth, through coaching, counselling, team building activities, cultural change and co-creation.

Once she was one of two co-founders and director of a company in business services which flourished in 13 years to a company with 80 staff members.

With her multicultural, medical, scientific, financial and holistic background, she can tailor a program that combines insight and integration with diagnostics and healing.

Her vision is: 'man is a unique and versatile creature, with deep answers for a happy life.'

For more information:
Email: info@heliotropo.nl
www.heliotropo.nl

The Fire Within

Malin Hedlund

Disappointed

My company is reorganizing. I am listening to a colleague talk about how it is going to be run, who will be responsible for what, and all the changes that will take place. Many of my coworkers are asked to leave the company, yet I get to stay and under conditions that are unfair. Actually they are outrageous! What about my ten years of experience as a coach and facilitator at a training company for leadership and personal development? Customer satisfaction? My skills and ability to influence and transform people's lives? Every single one of my coaching programs during the past years have drawn more participants, and yet I'm not chosen as a partner?

A cloud of anger, devastation, frustration and disappointment hovers over me. Even though I don't say anything aloud, inside I am SCREAMING. From the outside I may look like I am calm, but inside, there is a storm raging.

I make the decision to leave the company. It hurts. It's like saying goodbye to a dear friend or a loved one. These feelings are deep and complicated because it is where my career officially started. However my gut tells me it's time to move on.

Tired

It's an unusually hot day in Malmö and I am about to deliver a corporate presentation training. This is one of many trainings sessions away from home. These days, I am constantly on the road on my way to another client.

I carelessly, read the evaluation forms after the course, the participants gave high scores and are still delighted with my effort. Standing there, I am not very impressed with myself because this is the response I usually receive. They feel that my expertise has moved them forward. Their feedback does not affect me, so I think, *This is what I do. This is what they expect from a professional leadership coach and I am there for them, not for me.*

Why do I feel this way? I love what I do but not how I do it. Coaching brings me joy seeing people develop and thrive. However at the end of the day, what do *I* get out of it? My life feels repetitive, like a train, running on its tracks, moving forward but never changing course.

A few weeks later, I prepare for an in-house corporate training. I'm not in a good mood although I've just come back from a long run. My legs were stiff and my breathing was labored. I never got into the flow. I still pushed myself, because that's how I do things. Running is a way for me to relax, recharge, and meditate. But all it did this morning was stress me out and wind me up.

After the run, I set up my laptop, hoping to get some work done but my brain will not cooperate. I keep having to start over, rewrite, revise, and delete copy. I've now lost my train of thought. Anxiousness starts to creep up on me. *What is wrong with me today?*

My tired mind tells me I need vacation. All I need to do is get through this one big delivery…

Although I am barely prepared for the delivery, I exceed all expectations. Finally reaching that long awaited four-week vacation. Relaxation is high on the priority list, but spending time with my family comes first. I like to tell my clients that vacations are for recharging your batteries, for doing things that energize you, and that you enjoy doing.

Yet, somehow I am not able to apply this advice to myself. During my time off, I am restless, irritated and have too little energy to be social and invite people over. I have even less motivation to cook or clean. As if the situation could not get any worse, it ends up being the rainiest summer in years. Life would be so easy and stress-free if I could just get a few hours in the sun every day. A much needed trip to Crete is decided. Finally some rest!

I dread the day I have to go back to work again - really not looking forward to getting back into normal routines and busy days, which is very unlike me because I am usually enthusiastic and excited about new things.

During the first week of work, we have a series of off-site meetings to plan for the coming year. The very first day during the break, a colleague says, "Malin, I don't recognize you. What's wrong?" Out of nowhere I start to cry. All the feelings that have built up inside me during the past months are coming out. I knew I had to make a change in my life for a while now, but I'd been procrastinating.

Wiping away my tears, I try to focus on the meeting but I can't think, talk, or focus, much less answer the questions from my colleagues or boss. Instead I let all the irritation, loneliness, and frustration out in my tears. All of a sudden, I say to myself, "I can't live like this anymore."

My whole life I have tried to live up to be dependable, someone you can count on no matter what. I have always been that person who CAN and WILL do whatever it takes to get the job, project, assignment done. Even if I didn't like what I was doing or feel I had the talent or skills to adequately do it. Yet, no one has called me out as a fraud. But I am exhausted. It's so tiring being someone else all the time while pretending it's really your true self.

Later that day, my boss tells me I should take another three weeks off. He understands the seriousness of my current state. Relief washes over me. Feeling so thankful that he listens to me and is willing to help me battle my confusion.

Those three weeks turn into three months. It takes three months to get back on track.

Insights

I am nervous and feel a little uncomfortable. Normally I am the one asking questions, listening, supporting, and helping. Today, I find myself on the other side of the table. A woman greets me with a warm, friendly smile. She is a kind of a teacher and I've been meeting with her to try to understand what is going on in my life. She is calm and caring – I feel better already. She informs me that although I have no energy, appetite or self-confidence, I'm not depressed, I'm burned out.

Our meetings have had a positive impact on me. She makes me question myself and understand what, how, and why I should change my current situation. I feel safe and listened to.

Another realization I come to during this process is that I am not responsible for other people's actions. My job is to guide them in the right direction so they can make a decision about what to do and to take action. Was I really thinking that their results are a direct connection to my ability and skills? Did I really believe that I'm essentially the one determining the outcome of their lives? All these years I've been walking around thinking that it was my fault when a client failed in achieving their goals.

Looking back at my life, I realize that there is a pattern to everything I do. I push myself, because I am NOT a quitter. Ever since I made the decision to become a gymnast at seven years old, despite talent or the body for it, I have always demonstrated my capability of going beyond the limit.

The next thing she tells me has a profound impact on my transformational journey. She looks me in the eyes and says, "You have to prioritize YOURSELF first, then you can take care of those around you. If YOU are not in a balanced mental state, your loved ones will be negatively affected too." This hits me hard. I feel my eyes stinging and burning. Tears roll down my cheeks as I think about my daughter's current health – the stress she is going through. My fragile little angel with blond, curly hair and ocean blue eyes. So strong on the outside yet so vulnerable. The way in which she is trying to control the uncertainty she is feeling inside, she is just like me. My heart is aching.

What am I doing? Harming myself and my family like that. Saying yes to any job opportunity to prove myself worthy, and putting my clients before myself, my lovely husband, and my precious children? I am angry and ashamed. This hits me hard, like a punch in the face. I decide take action and change my way of life.

It's like a wonder – as soon as I start acting different, taking care of myself, give myself some time to recharge, read, and meditate, my daughter also starts to feel better. It is as if I reached a crossroads and am forced to choose a different path. We start spending more time together at home, and I learn to say no to jobs. It is a truly wonderful feeling.

Starting my business

Now that I have this new insight about my life, I have finally realized what I want to do next. Most people would call me crazy, starting my own business in the middle of a recession, but I'm convinced it's the right thing to do. I can't go back to where I was.

Just thinking about having my own business makes me want to sing and dance. My two biggest passions, *physical/ inner strength and personal leadership development*, are what I will be working with.

Despite the fact that I have barely started working, I feel free, rich, and happy. The feeling of owning my calendar and working with areas that are close to my heart is indescribable. After quite a tough start, financially I am on a great journey. And I have so much to do, once again. Yet, this time it's rewarding rather than only stressful. At a certain point, I am so busy that I need to hire somebody to help me run the business.

This is when my husband comes home and tells me he got an offer to move abroad. We agree that this is an adventure we cannot pass up. I decide to continue my business in the Netherlands, where we'll be moving.

Starting Again

So I find myself in a new country, where I don't know anybody, have no clients or contacts, and absolutely no idea where or how to start working on my business. I'm losing my confidence. Feeling lost, I start questioning myself again. Who am I? Who do I want to be? Essentially, I am a stay-at-home mom more than anything else. What is my worth? What do I actually know? Who would want to hire me?

To get out of the self-pity and anxiety regarding my business, I decide to set up some goals and challenges for myself. I need something to force me out of my comfort zone, something that fulfills me. I decide that a marathon, will be my focus. Running such a long distance requires not only physical, but also mental capacity and strength. It becomes a game changer for my everyday life *and* my business. Training for this race turns out to be a new start. It gives me a fresh perspective, clarity, and rituals that I need to stick to in order to build strength and endurance for the race.

I see a huge improvement in myself when it comes to positive thinking. Every single running session also works as a mental strength training – some days are so tough that I need a mantra to get through my runs. If I can strengthen my mindset and attitude in combination with other skills, I can mold my life in any way I want. This knowledge leaves me feeling powerful. I truly believe this to be a great recipe for living your most authentic life – building up mental and physical strength.

Perseverance, my absolute strongest companion, was also my worst enemy. It led me to a burnout. After living so many years in a constant race to prove myself, I have finally come to understand the importance of using my inner power and not only my external achievement. In the end, perseverance has been my best buddy, and it has taught me so much.

My life would not have been the same without it. Perseverance has shaped me into who I am today and given me the experiences I have been through. It used to put me in mental and physical fatigue. Today, I know when and how to use it to become stronger.

Reward

I find myself in the front row, feeling excited but calm, not worried about how I'll perform or what anyone will think of me. I breathe in deeply, and then out. This fills me with new energy and inspiration. During this event, I will be one of the main speakers. When I hear my name called a feeling of joy rushed over me. As I walk on stage, I allow myself to take a moment to embrace the silence in the audience. I feel powerful despite the fact that there are twice as many spectators as I had expected.

My speech puts me in a mindful state. I receive warm, appreciative feedback and it makes me beyond delightful to hear these comments. People tell me I have inspired them to take action and start working on their dreams and goals. This time I used my passion, and it feels wonderful.

Reflections

Today, I am aware of my inner wisdom and listen to the signals my body gives me. Burning out gave me insight into the obstacles that can be in the way of achieving success and happiness. I live in the now, and focus on what I can change right in this moment rather than what I will be doing or changing two days from now. Instead of putting my thoughts on autopilot, I ask myself insightful and important questions that will make me think. It challenges me in a powerful way.

We all have talents, traits, strengths, and gifts, but many of us do not know how to use them. I have learned to unleash them and use them in my favor. However selfish it may sound, I prioritize myself FIRST. When I am my best self, I am so much more valuable to those around me, and that is how I live my most authentic life. When you acknowledge and draw out your inner resources and strengths, you WILL thrive! This is a very important concept to me, and it changed everything.

Your turn:

Are you clear about what makes your heart sing?
What is your biggest obstacle?
How are you planning to live your most authentic life?

About the Author

Malin Hedlund, owner of MH Leadership, is a passionate Personal Leadership coach and engaging facilitator, working with individuals and teams. She is an expert in personal development, inspiring success in others through a combination of one on one and team coaching and promotion of a healthy and active lifestyle. Her focus is working with ambitious female leaders.

Malin has multiple years of international experience and she is also a certified Personal Fitness Trainer.

Find out more about Malin Hedlund at www.mhleadership.com
Connect with Malin on these social networks:
www.linkedin.com/in/malinhedlund
www.facebook.com/MHLeadership

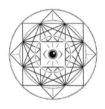

Part 2
When Peace Surpasses Understanding

Sometimes life's circumstances leave us feeling such anguish that peace can seem like a distant land or far away planet. And the yearning we feel to return to a place of serenity, can be as intense as the pain a jilted lover feels, aching for their beloved to bestow once again, an affectionate glance in their direction.

When we are struck with a devastating blow we didn't see coming, or the rug of life is unexpectedly ripped from beneath us, we may be faced with a sickening sense of vulnerability and loneliness. And at those times, despite trying all that we know to do, things just aren't working, or we run out of willing allies, we may need the helping hand of an angel to see us through the darkness. We may even need an infusion of power from the very Source of all life to enable us to pick ourselves up and move forward.

I've personally endured those types of painful lows and dark days, not knowing if I had the strength or desire to go on. Sometimes the way out of a dim cave of confusion and loss came through supernatural deliverance. Experience has shown me that the grace, love and support of the Divine is ours for the asking in our time of need.

When you open up to receive it, you may become a witness to an out of this world ability to transcend pain and suffering. In fact, you may even be delivered to a state of such wondrous bliss that you won't be able to understand how joy, and the chaos of life, could co-exist.

The tragedies of mass casualties, suicide, physical illness, and personal loss, touch each of us in one way or another. The stories in Part 2 demonstrate, that in spite of the senselessness of these situations, we are surrounded by love, peace and angelic support.

Angels Are Among Us

Karena Virginia

In 2001 New York City was in the midst of the 9/11 attack. My husband, who is a lawyer near the financial district, was in his office doing the work he always does. Just a regular day, only the weather was exceptionally beautiful and the air extra crisp. It was almost a surreal morning. Our daughter was six weeks old, and I was breastfeeding her and feeling a loneliness that I was too ashamed to share with others. I adored my husband. He was truly my soulmate and my dream come true. I waited my whole life for him, and we were only married for a little over a year. Our daughter Gabriella was the greatest gift in the world. She was my dream come true.

However, as an empath, there was a weight on me. An emptiness in my stomach that made no sense to me logically. It was most likely postpartum depression, but as a yogi I thought I could overcome it naturally.

As a child I used to see angels. I thought everybody saw them until one day in church I mentioned it to my Sunday school teacher who then looked at me strangely. After that, I learned to keep my angels private until they stopped visiting. I had turned away from them because I felt shame for being so different than my best friend who seemed perfect in every way. Alison lived across the street from my childhood home. She had gorgeous curly blonde hair and sparkly blue eyes, and she always said the perfect things. The older neighbors loved her, and they often made fun of me, or worse just ignored me.

I felt like I was far from perfect. I was tall and awkward. I often said really odd things. Teachers ignored me. And I often retreated into daydreams as a way to cope with an inexplicable sadness my soul carried.

I found yoga practice when I was eighteen in college. It was not popular in the early 1990's, but it was my therapy. I loved it, and practiced meditation daily. Yoga was my path to the divine, and it was the avenue back to the angels.

Sometimes days would feel heavy for me, but I always found my way to my yoga mat and music. Having a baby makes it more challenging to find time for ourselves, and with the hormonal changes I was experiencing, I was simply cranky. Verrrry cranky.

Looking back I know it was a collective heaviness brought on by the tragedy that had befallen so many souls on that tragic day.

On September 11, 2001 I woke up with a longing I can't fully explain. It was not the normal postnatal pang or exhaustion. It was a heaviness that felt like a heavy weight on my heart. I had to drag myself out of bed, and I felt such a sense of shame for not being able to get through such a sadness.

My husband and I had been married for 14 months and known one another for two years. We lived in a beautiful house. But it was filled with a longing that I could not understand. I was surrounded by love in our dream house as my dream husband slept next to me with our beautiful baby snuggled between us. My longing really confused me. The emptiness in my core that felt like a pang of pain, which brought about a waterfall of tears that morning.

My sister-in-law called me as I was slowly peeling a mango in the kitchen. My hands were sticky and I carried Gabriella in a sling over my heart. I did not have an appetite, but made it a discipline to eat. My sister-in-law's voice was filled with concern when she asked, "Is Chuck at work?" That's the moment my heart fell. I knew from her voice that something was very wrong, and turning the television on just confirmed the horror.

The world trade center had been hit. My husband's office was there. This can't be real, I thought. This must be a nightmare, I screamed out to the empty house. It got worse. The second tower was hit, and then they both collapsed. I watched them collapse on the TV. It was the most horrific site, and we all thought the entire area surrounding the towers was done for. My husband. Gone. My life.... never the same.

He is gone. Just like that. In an instant, and his toothbrush is still wet. What was wrong with me? I didn't appreciate him enough. I thought we had an entire life together. I was such a brat the night before. I was complaining about something so trivial. My sensitivity to life exacerbated everything all the time, and I was never happy. What was wrong with me? Why did I feel everything so much all the time.

A sensation of extreme regret and shame came over me and my skin began to burn. The burning on my skin has always been part of my increased sensitivity. There is no way to explain how difficult it feels when you are an empath.

I called him. No answer.

I could not function. My body was literally paralyzed in trauma. The phones were not working. An entire day of fear, regret, horror, sadness, guilt, grief and doubt shook my body. Shivers and pain. A little innocent baby in my arms and a longing that made the pit in my stomach from the morning seem like a distant and trivial memory.

Chuck came home hours later.

"Don't touch me. I'm full of chemicals and debris," he said.

He threw his suit in the garbage and took the bag outside, and that's when I realized what he meant. Debris covered his clothing. His eyes looked different. They were empty. He had changed in that instant. But, he was home. I could handle anything else. He was home, and so many weren't home.

Shock, shame, sadness along with a sense of relief washed over me. I cooked. I cleaned. I asked him questions. I did everything I could think of to make him feel better about the trauma he had certainly just experienced. But he needed to be alone.

I took Gabriella upstairs, put her to sleep, and I started to meditate and pray. And soon tears were rolling down my cheeks. It felt like I was crying for thousands of people. Then a feeling of overwhelming love washed over me. I wanted to save everyone. I wanted to help, serve humanity and love. I wanted to open my heart and give everything I could to the world. A powerful and energy came over me, and my body felt like it was as light as a feather.

That's when it happened. I looked through the window into the sunny afternoon and I saw them. Angels. The same ones I saw as a child. However, this time there were thousands.

Why would such a profound peace come over me at this moment? How could I feel a sense of hope in the midst of hundreds of families feeling the trauma of the events that shook the country?

What I was seeing were the new angels who were crossing over and the ancient angels who were inviting them to heaven.

My mind needed to find stillness to fully experience the grace and beauty in front of me.

"Keep us a secret for now," I heard them say. "They will not understand yet. You must bring them love and light. Just show up," they said.

Angels are among us.

Many of us who are super sensitive to life are actually highly sensitive to the healing ability of heaven as well. It is when we re-frame our shame around feeling so vulnerable and dramatic into self-love for caring so deeply that we see the gift of sensitivity.

Angels are always with us. In the moments when we are petri-fied or grieving, they show up in an instant. We do not always see them, but we do not need to. When we inhale the love of the an-gelic into our hearts and we exhale the pain of life out of our cells, we know they are the ones doing the work.

May these words touch your heart and remind you of the light that lives all around you every moment of every single day. At this time, life in our world feels so chaotic, but the coziness of heaven is just a breath away.

Bless you.

About the Author

Karena Virginia is an inspirational speaker and healer who brings deep spiritual mysticism to the modern world in a cozy and embracing style. Karena shares kundalini yoga and spiritual practices to heal the trauma that resides in our energy bodies and allow the love from our hearts to shine forth so we can live a life of fulfillment, happiness, and health.

Karena is a member of Oprah Winfrey's Belief team, and her passion is to bring the technology of ancient and miraculous healing to the masses as seen in her highly acclaimed yoga video, "The Power of Kundalini Yoga," the popular "Relax and Attract" App and her latest book, *Essential Kundalini Yoga*, which is bringing light and transformation into the hearts of many people around the world.

Connect with Karena at www.KarenaVirginia.com

Twists and Turns May Make Me Learn, But Patience Never Fails Me

Karin Eke

It has been a bumpy ride to say the least over these past few years. I had been meandering through life, as if pre-programmed like a robot to be the perfect little child who never stepped out of line, then the perfect little wife and mother, tending to everyone's needs and doing her best not to tread on anyone's toes or hurt anyone's feelings. I was therefore taken aback and completely shaken up when a revolution started within our home in 2012. It was time for me to wake up and wake up I did!

The tumultuous ride probably started for me back in 2001 when I was pregnant with my second child. I loved being pregnant and felt so alive and excited about the birth of a baby boy. I had been gifted with a girl and now a boy and was feeling so grateful. This beautiful state of being stopped temporarily in May 2001.

One evening after work, I had a hospital appointment for an amniocentesis, a screening process in which a needle is inserted into the womb to sample the fluid surrounding the fetus. I'd had gestational diabetes during my first pregnancy, so I thought this was just another one of the many routine check-ups. The lady doctor we saw was the head of the department and was a very efficient, no-nonsense type of person, so we were called in on time for the exam.

Different feelings had been bubbling away during the lead up to this moment of truth. I was immediately impressed by the size of the needle that was about to be poked inside me, but too excited to find out more about the new life that was forming inside me to let it torment me. Having been warned of the potential consequences if the needle touched the wrong places, I just wanted it to be over as quickly as possible. All of these feelings faded away into insignificance however when the doctor bluntly announced that there was a problem with the baby's heart and in all likelihood more than one anomaly.

"I am going to refer you to the number one paediatric cardiologist in Paris," she continued curtly. My heart stopped, I broke out in a cold sweat and a multitude of questions sprang to mind. A deathly silence was present within me then, lo and behold, there was a power outage and the screen went black, all the lights went out and everything became silent.

I started to panic as there I was, stranded, lying with a great big needle stuck in my womb. All the surrounding noises had stopped. There were no more beeping machines in the background, and the absence of noise was deadly. As tears rolled down my cheeks, the doctor was no doubt explaining how she was not in a position to elaborate on the condition. I did my best to listen, but I was no longer there.

My son had open-heart surgery at birth. For the next few years, my focus and first concern was caretaking and nursing him back to health. 'Head down and get on with it' could have easily been my motto. The years passed by with their ups and downs, joys and challenges, but I was living a lie. I was not happy and didn't even realise it. I was completely disconnected from my feelings. To the outside world I must have seemed happy. I was married, had two lovely children, we went on holiday most years, and we were financially stable. However, I was nowhere in the picture. Non-existent. I had put my life to one side and I had forgotten to dream.

My marriage was gradually becoming less and less exciting, the feelings of dissatisfaction and boredom were creating a chronic sadness inside me. I don't even recall how I ended up on the floor one evening in the autumn of 2009. I just remember sitting on the cold tiles with my back against the sofa and my husband sitting close by. I'm not even sure what had brought me to the breaking point. The children were in bed, all was calm, yet I was feeling miserable. So miserable and disheartened that suicidal thoughts fleetingly crossed my mind.

I desperately tried to tell my husband how I was feeling but the words remained stuck in my throat. I was again so frustrated at not being able to express myself and to top it all, there was absolutely no response from him to the few words that I managed to get out. All I could feel was a concrete wall of indifference, there was no love, not even a tiny inkling of emotion. I felt a pang in my heart and realised at that moment that I was on my own. A feeling of loneliness welled up inside me. I stared at the picture on the wall in front of me, a photo with a beautiful blue sky, clear blue water, sparkling white sand, and I just knew I had to find a way back to happiness, back to myself.

And in that moment of darkness, I decided I was going to do whatever it took to get myself out of there.

A couple of months later, my son was due for his first angiogram, an X-ray detailing the arteries of his heart. He was 8 years old and I was worried about the psychological impact that a huge scar from the neck down after his open-heart surgery could have, so I asked the head of department at the hospital for her advice.

She thought it was a great question, but didn't know how to answer it, so invited me to contact their team of psychologists. Reluctantly, we did just that, and how grateful I was that we did.

The psychologist we were assigned turned out to be the most amazing person I have ever met.

From the moment our first appointment was set down in the diary, I felt a deep connection to her. It was unlike anything I had ever experienced before. It was as if an immediate, intense bond had been established between us and I felt as though we had found a safe place where I would finally be heard. I was completely dumbfounded as before we even met, I felt energy swirling all around me and I just knew that this was it! A change was happening and our lives were about to be transformed. The magic had begun and at last my prayers had been answered. Feelings of utter relief coupled with excitement came over me.

I realised that she was definitely not your 'ordinary' therapist and wondered if she had a magic wand up her sleeve. I had been captivated and the weekly meeting with my son seemed to be more exciting for me than it was for him, even though I only saw the therapist for a few minutes after each session. In just these few minutes, it became clear that the work she was doing enabled thoughts, feelings and emotions to emerge naturally. I felt alive, energised, euphoric and excited about what these sessions were going to bring to the family. How I could be affected without even having to be there was beyond me at the time!

My life started to revolve around these weekly appointments. I could feel the magic happening on a quantum level and became aware of the healing effect that words can have. This really was eye-opening as my son was having the counselling and I was feeling immediate benefits in my body! I felt lighter as what seemed like layers of suffering were lifting off, spiralling off into no-where, as if all the energetic charge from the past was simply leaving my space. My heart was breaking open and new light was coming in. My life was transforming at the same time as my son's was!

Without a shadow of a doubt, I was being reconnected to higher states of consciousness and I knew that what I was experiencing was precisely what I wanted to create in my own life: to bring transformation, magic, and healing to others through intention and presence. This revelation was so exciting, that I woke up every day for the next few months feeling immense joy and gratitude. Ideas came to me and felt like streams of energy running through me. This is what life is all about, I thought, as all my senses were aroused and awakened. I was alert to everything that was going on within and around me and I was not going to miss a thing, it was far too exciting!

I spent a lot of time laughing as I was simply amazed at what was happening. I started dropping objects or tripping over things, basically having many experiences which pushed me into realising they were the immediate boomerang effect of my self-sabotaging thoughts. This was such a game changer and was just the beginning! Synchronicities became an every-day experience and repeated number patterns were showing up on clocks in perfect alignment with the positive thoughts and ideas that were coming to me. I just had to think of people and I would run into them on the street or they happened to call me at that moment.

I even felt at one with the weather! The sun magically started to shine whenever I was thinking about someone and feeling love for them. It would also start to rain in perfect alignment with thoughts that I wanted to wash away. I had no idea at the time that my vibrational frequency had increased and I had stepped into a new dimension; I was just reveling in the feeling of being at one with the universe and connected to something far greater than me.

I was in a permanent elated state for months. The relationship with my husband improved, harmony came back into the family and it seemed as if we were all in the flow of life. I felt such gratitude to have been able to lift the veil of darkness and I felt unstoppable. I was on a quest and I was desperate to share it with the world as I so wanted everyone to experience these intense feelings and daily miraculous occurrences. It was truly life-changing to realise that I was attracting different circumstances into my life through thinking and feeling differently.

In 2010, we decided to go on holiday to Scotland and had planned to stay a couple of days at my parents' house in the north of England to break up the long car ride from Paris. We arrived late one Saturday evening in August, feeling happy and relaxed as we had had a smooth journey and we were all enjoying each other's company. To my astonishment, the children suddenly appeared, ready for bed and what's more surprising, eager to go.

I was no longer there though, as I had become an observer in the room. I had come out of my body and was in a timeless, limitless space of expansiveness. Participating in the fun, joy and laughter of a family gathering that exceeded any level of happiness that we had previously experienced did however surprise me as I recall pinching myself at one point to check if this was real. I was definitely there! This sounds like a fairy tale, right? Well, it was and lasted for 36 hours. My logical brain had been put on hold and I had been taken over by a feeling of pure love, joy, expansion and compassion. I had awakened to something greater.

Monday morning came and we set off for Scotland on a beautiful summer's day. The sun was shining and I was basking in the beauty of everything that surrounded me. All of a sudden, I was struck by an intense feeling of fear. At that moment, I came with a thud back into my body. It was as if my consciousness had returned into my body as soon as fear had set in.

In 2012 I really didn't understand what was going on as things started going pear-shaped. There was absolutely no way of going back to the old way of thinking and being once I'd had such an experience. I felt on top of the world and thought that it was possible to overcome any challenge. Thank goodness I had learned what inner peace, unconditional love and universal flow truly felt like as it was as if this had been preparing me for what was to come.

At the end of 2013 and in the midst of a traumatic divorce, I was magnetised through the internet to a beautiful energy healing modality called Quantum Touch, a practice which activates the body's subtle energies to remove blocks and stimulate its inherent ability to heal itself. I could feel energy flowing through me again, immediately signed up for the online course and loved it so much, I attended the first live workshop shortly after.

The Monday morning following the workshop, I excitedly decided to practise one of the techniques I had just learned and sitting comfortably at home, closed my eyes and began to run energy. When I opened my eyes, I was astounded. My hands had disappeared! All I could see was energy and a soft purple colour in places. I shook my head, disbelieving what I saw, turned my head away and looked back. Still no hands! My feelings of awe and wonder came to a stop when fear set in and my hands magically rematerialised. I then realised that my own fears had jolted me out of this experience, recalling my out-of-body experience in 2010 and how fear had brought me back into my body back then.

Another miraculous, spontaneous experience was soon to follow. I had attended a workshop on youthing and learning ways to regenerate our body's cells. Without doing anything consciously however, I suddenly found myself one day in a younger body! I had no blemishes or wrinkles on my skin, the few white hairs I had had disappeared, it was as if I had regenerated myself! I was so amazed, I frantically kept going back to the mirror to check if it was real! As soon as fear and doubt set in however, I was brought back to my former self, the more familiar way of being.

I yearned to share these amazing discoveries of human potential with others. It was yet more proof that we are so much more than a physical body and have unlimited power. This now fuels my mission today to help others achieve just the same or better. Just imagine how the world would be if we all had young, vibrant, healthy bodies!

My journey these past few years has taught me a lot about the deeper truths of what we are actually living and how all our experiences are calling us to something greater and more in alignment with our true essence. The fact that I have experienced the Divine picking me up through challenging moments, I have learnt to trust in the end result and always believe in myself, everything being a side-effect of the connection with myself. I feel so grateful that my path is often embellished with spontaneous, magical healing experiences.

Interestingly, in French, the word magic, la magie, is the phonetic equivalent of '*l'âme agit*', loosely translated as the soul is speaking. Now that I know that everything in the universe is perfectly orchestrated and that everything in my life is a gift, I am able to unwrap presents every day, and that is what I want for you so that you can discover your own true self. May you all be blessed with inner peace and find your own magic wand as your wish is your command!

About the Author

Karin is a Lightworker, mystic, energy healer, and empath. After profoundly transformational experiences in 2010, she caught glimpses of her Higher Self and saw that it is possible to put a stop to all pain and suffering in the world. She opened up to infinite human potential, realised that magic is all around us and committed to becoming a true vibrational catalyst in order to help raise the vibration of the planet and empower others on their ascension path.

Karin now helps people to deeply connect with their Higher Self in order to create a life of unconditional love, flow, and inner peace.

To connect with Karin:
Email: karin.eke@free.fr
Tel : +33783520047
www.theascensionpath.com

You can also find Karin on Facebook and Instagram:
www.facebook.com/karinm.eke
www.facebook.com/groups/985205621653689
www.instagram.com/karin_eke

I Am Home

Halina Goldstein

People often tell me that my voice is so loving that it makes them feel at peace. But my life has not always been peaceful or loving. On the contrary, it was filled with loss. Early on, I lost the closeness of a mother, I lost friends, family, home country, language, and I lost any sense of belonging. I felt lonely even before I had a word for it.

When I was in my twenties and thirties I was convinced that if I could find someone to love me then everything would get better. I would feel supported, safe, and seen, I would be happy. So while it may have seemed that I was happy with my work, and was thriving spiritually and creatively (I worked as a semi-professional musician back then), underneath it all there was always the search for 'the one'. But I was always searching and never finding what I was looking for.

My relationships kept ending and each time, the feeling of loneliness grew even more. I tried to do something about it, with therapy, healing, massage and so many other holistic approaches. But even if there were good days, loneliness would always return.

Some days it made me feel cold, numb and completely depleted. Other days it was like a hunger for love, so painful I couldn't stand it. This was one such day. I was lying on the floor and I had been crying so much that there wasn't an ounce of energy left in me. It was like being wounded and near death, begging for help, but nobody came. I lay there, waiting for it to end.

Suddenly, I didn't feel alone. It was as if someone was there with me! I felt so loved, so embraced… and the room was lit with a bright light! Although the curtains were drawn, it was as if the sun was shining inside the room. The light was filling the space and expanding beyond it, and it was changing me. I was becoming one with its sweet, loving presence. I was one with everything and everyone, the entire world, the endless universe. There was nothing but love. Everything fell into place, everything was so right, there was only joy.

I don't know how much time passed this way. This blissful feeling followed me for the rest of the day. That night I fell asleep with peace in my heart.

The next day I woke up to my normal reality. The feeling of love wasn't there anymore. Neither was the overwhelming need for it. But after a few days loneliness returned. Having just experienced a miraculous shift from loneliness to love I thought I'd be able to manage it now, that I'd somehow find my way back into bliss. But I couldn't.

In the following months, from time to time the loving presence would come back, always out of the blue, then disappear again, leaving me with no idea how to make love stay. And so I continued my search for someone to love me.

Then one late afternoon, after a day-long spiritual conference, I was on my way home. As always, after spending time with many people, the feeling of being alone was even stronger, and my thoughts were circling around the same old question: "Where is that someone for me?" Only this time I was honest with myself. *You have been in all kinds of relationships, with men and with women, and none of it worked out. You're 42. Who do you think you're fooling?*

In that moment, for the first time ever, I faced the truth. I'm meant to be alone. But I still need love! Where do I find it then? I wondered. Making my way down a busy Copenhagen street, I suddenly stopped. I got an answer. Love must be in me. I have loved and that means I am capable of love. What if I could love myself the way I can love someone else?

This was the beginning of my self-love practice. It was surprisingly easy. I became committed to loving everything that I was. Whatever I didn't like about myself, I was learning to love. I listened to my needs and I gave myself what I needed. I deliberately did for myself everything I would do for a beloved. I said loving words to myself. I bought flowers and gifts for myself. I made food for myself and savored it the way I would with a lover. I danced with myself.

It worked! I started feeling better and better, more and more fulfilled in my own company. Within a year I literally fell in love with myself! It was a similar experience to falling in love with someone else. I was having a loving, intimate, happy relationship with myself, body and soul.

Everything changed. I brought my newfound happiness into everything I did. My music became warmer, my spirituality higher, my friendships more open. I was kinder with other people than ever before, I saw our similarities more than our differences. I had a new sense of belonging wherever I went.

I painted a big picture with the words "I am home" on it and put it up on my wall. I truly had arrived. I *was* my home. My search was over and I didn't need anything more to happen. But of course, that was when something happened.

While I was sitting in meditation one day, out of nowhere I saw an image of a popular Danish New Age musician. It felt insisting somehow, yet I had no idea what the image was trying to tell me so I left it at that. But over the next few days, 5 different people, friends, and even strangers reached out to me for unrelated reasons. During those conversations they all said the same: "You should meet this man."

So I wrote him a letter. "Hi, my name is Halina and you showed up in my meditation. I don't know what it means but I assume it has something to do with music. Maybe we should meet one day and try to play together?" I mailed it then forgot all about it because I didn't expect an answer.

He later told me that when he found the letter in his mailbox he held the envelope in his hands and smiled for no apparent reason. He often received requests from people who wanted to play with him and he would reject them all, but with me it was different. He called me right away and invited me to visit him in his studio.

We met and there was an instant warm openness between us. We sat down to play (he with his guitar and keyboards, I with my silver flutes). We agreed to not prepare the music at all, just wait and see what happened, if anything. Then the first notes sounded, and they were in perfect harmony! From there we played whatever we felt inspired to. It was as if we were playing from a score. It was magical.

We fell in love with each other as well, immediately, and connected beautifully in every way, body and spirit, feelings and thoughts. We spent as much time together as we could and when we couldn't we would talk on the phone for hours. After a couple of weeks he asked me to move in with him. It was as if we had known each other forever already. And yet, I hesitated.

Yes, part of me just wanted to be in this flow with him. But there was also the other side of me. I had just found happiness within myself and I didn't want to lose that. I also had a sense that I was to embark on a deeper spiritual journey that required me to live alone. I had found what I had been craving for so many years yet, I was at a crossroads.

What made me choose one road rather than the other was the fact that I had never been in a relationship like this one before. I didn't want to die without having had that experience. So, I moved in with him. We married within less than a year and I loved it.

There was so much we could share with each other. A home, the beautiful nature around us, deep soul to soul conversations, a tantric like intimacy, a passion for music and creativity... Every morning I would wake up and look at him sleeping by my side, and feel so grateful for the ways he made me happy!

There were times however when he would suddenly shut down, for no apparent reason. I would feel the enormous tension in him but he refused to speak with me, about that or anything else. Or when he did talk it was as if he were a stranger. I was hurting, for him and for me, and couldn't understand what was happening. I had thoughts of leaving him.

But I had a deep loyalty towards love itself. If this is what love called me to deal with then I would stay and deal with it, even if it was painful. And so I did. Then, after a few days, as unexpected as when he got distant, he would return to his sweet old self and we would be back in harmony.

Years passed this way, but then something started to change. After one of his down periods he said he couldn't be creative with me in the house, he needed his own space. To support his work, even if reluctantly, I moved out.

We continued being together for a few more years, and at one point I even moved back to the house. But our relationship wasn't the same. Among other things, I was exploring a spiritual approach that questioned the very nature of the physical reality. I found it liberating. It helped me see how we can meet any of life's challenges with trust. He however found it deeply provoking, especially when it came to financial matters. So much so that it eventually became his reason for wanting a divorce.

Once again, I was losing everything that was dear to me. What were but short episodes previously became the new normal; my soulmate turned into a stranger, and a heartless one at times. I was confronted with a choice. Would I close my heart like he did or would I, even while divorcing him, honor the love that brought us together to begin with? I chose love.

I found a tiny studio for myself. The day I moved in I got very ill, and had a high fever. I left the boxes unpacked, lay down on a mattress on the floor and went to sleep. That's how I spent the following days. Morning after morning I'd wake up crying, or angry, or just empty. All I wanted was sleep.

Until, one morning, I woke up... and I was completely happy! It didn't make any sense. Nothing around me had changed, the mess was still there, yet I was in pure joy! I thought, *This must be my intuition telling me something wonderful is to happen today!* All day I was waiting for something special to happen, but nothing did. The next day again I woke up to joy, and again I spent all day waiting for something to happen that would explain it.

It took a few days like this before I finally acknowledged that I was in joy and there was no external reason for it whatsoever. I also realized that it wasn't my ex-husband who had made me so happy during the time we had together. It was the joy and the love within me. It was wonderful that we could share it, and sharing it with him made it truly extraordinary and magical. But the joy and the love itself came from within.

I had returned to myself and also to the path that I did not take at the crossroads 9 years earlier. I was living alone, in joy, and my exploration of the inner realm took me further still. It was taking me into such deep experiences, and such deep desire to live my truth wholeheartedly… But there was also fear.

To overcome it I needed to know that what I relied on was indeed real and true and not just an illusion. But how could I be certain of it? The only way was to discard everything I had ever learned about spirituality. When all my spiritual ideas were gone, when I was left with nothing but my own experience, what truth would I be left with, if any? That was the question, and for three days, it sent me into the dark night of the soul.

And then my soul responded. Out of the darkness emerged an inner connection so clear and so undeniable that it became the rock-solid foundation upon which I have built ever since. Feeling connected with my soul this way, I can trust my heart and my intuition. I can rely on the love and wisdom within me and share it with those I'm here to serve. I'm gradually awakening to more and more of what our reality truly is, more and more of the joy and oneness that is our birthright.

In this very moment, I see how everything is coming into existence. I see how waves of energy are becoming my body, they're becoming the things around me too. Waves of joy, curiosity, love, wonder, gratitude… My heart is overflowing.

Even as life feels magical, showering me with beautiful friends and adventures I didn't think possible... if you ask me, there is nothing more amazing, nothing more miraculous than this very moment. Everything we ever wanted, ever longed for, ever waited for, is already here, now.

It has been a long journey home.

I thought I was lonely because I was on my own, but I came to know that I was lonely because I had disowned myself.

I thought love was evading me and abandoning me, but I came to know that I had evaded and abandoned the love within me.

I thought that it would take a miracle for life to change to the better, but I came to know that everything is a miracle already, every single moment.

When we don't feel it or don't see it this way, it's because we're lost, in thinking or in some other kind of pain. But there is a way back into the light and the joy that is our true nature. I found it the hard way but you don't have to.

In this moment, I'm typing these letters, these words, these sentences, for you. In this moment, your eyes are seeing these letters, these words, these sentences. This is our shared miracle, right there, right now.

You are home too. Welcome home.

About the Author

Halina Goldstein is a spiritual speaker, teacher and mentor. She lives in Denmark and works globally. Halina is the founder of Awakening to Joyful Living at **www.HalinaGold.com**. Her mission is to help spiritual seekers shine their light more fully, live with purpose, and experience joy, love, and freedom in every area of their life. In our troubled world there is a tremendous need for a joyful, peaceful, balancing presence from as many people as possible.

To know more about her philosophy and learn a simple yet powerful joy practice download the "Finding Joy Every Day" e-book at **www.HalinaGold.com/welcome**.

Halina has also founded the Joy Keepers Network at

www.JoyKeepers.org, a movement dedicated to bringing more joy to the world. While the network is open to the great variety of spiritual approaches available today, members recognize joy and oneness as powerful, fundamental states available to every human being.

A Drastic Intervention

Caroline Hoek

As the after dinner laziness kicked in, I picked up a magazine a friend had given me the other day. Not really reading it I distractedly turned the pages as my mind wandered off. On one page however, my eyes were drawn to 'Retreat in Bali' and my heart skipped a beat. No, this can't be possible, it was about Ratu Bagus, the energy healer I visited over 10 years ago. I was wide awake now and curious as I read the story about a woman who went to his ashram. So it's called an ashram now, I thought, remembering when the sessions were being held in an old pigs' shed.

This little Balinese man, with powers I could not comprehend, had become famous! Whilst my eyes took in the words, my heart took hold of a longing. Could this be how I would finally get rid of the behaviour that has been bothering me (and not only me) for such a long time? Coming from a troubled background where addiction, abuse, and neglect have been part of my upbringing, the need to be in control was equally strong and tiresome. I smiled as I thought of my husband, Hans, who would surely congratulate me if I succeeded in letting go.

I went to Bali alone.

At the airport, the warm humid air wrapped around me like a blanket. The smell of kretek, the typical Indonesian cigarette stuffed with tobacco and cloves, welcomed me even more as I waited to collect my suitcase.

Surprisingly, my name was spelled correctly on the board the driver was holding. "Selamat datang, missis", he greeted me as we shook hands. "Terima kasih" I replied to his surprise. "Ah, you speaking Bahasa. Bagus!" But since this was not really the case, the two-hour drive could have been spent in silence if not for the constant comments he made to the people on the road. The hustle and bustle of scooters packed with whole families and even chickens, was, as always a delight. But as the day turned into evening and a deep blackness surrounded us, I was relieved when the driver announced we were almost there.

The ashram was situated on the sacred Mount Agung. A friendly woman showed me to my room and soon I was alone with only the sound of crickets and the funny mating call of the Tokay lizard. Tired from the long journey I decided to unpack tomorrow and after a short shower I fell into a dreamless sleep.

At 6:30 am the alarm went off, it would be my ritual for the next 2 weeks. I would wake up and shake my body for 6 hours a day, every day, I would experience the healing touch of Ratu Bagus. The sessions are supposed to release blocks and tune in to the power of love.

As I entered the ashram the small community I remembered from 10 years ago had turned into a little village. Small, single room houses alternated with 2 story ones. Some had balconies with elegantly shaped fences. Stone statues of the Hindu gods Ganesh and Hanuman, partly covered in cloth, gave this place an even more sacred feel. I was being welcomed by the blossoming Bougainville sharing her abundance of red flowers. Huge banana leaves heaved as if saying 'Hi, you can slow down your pace now', while a small monkey mirrored my curiosity.

Colourful slippers piled outside the Taman told me I was not the first to enter. The beat of the music lured me to dance and shake almost immediately. As I did I took in the lovely temple hall, decorated with more statues and flowers. There were buckets that could be used in case I had to vomit when releasing blocks. This would be my routine. Throughout the week I laughed and cried, slowly letting go. Sometimes Ratu's touch would evoke a tremendous shaking I could not control, feeling a deep relief afterwards. Once he only pointed at me from a distance and I felt I was pushed backwards with incredible force.

I knew that taking the sacred tobacco would be helpful to go even deeper. But just the thought of it filled me with sheer panic as images of my drunken father, and me as a little girl not allowed to show my feelings flashed in my mind. What if I lost control? What if I could let go? I longed to break free from feeling trapped by my past.

But on this morning, the moment I opened my eyes, I remembered the promise I made myself the day before; I would use the tobacco. This made me want to stay in bed, this comfortable bed with cool white sheets, gently caressing my body. In this quiet white room, where the wooden door is keeping the world at a safe distance, I wanted to stay. But outside I could already hear the faint sounds of people getting up and preparing for the next session. The clock was telling me I should do the same. My inner voice was telling me I should do the same. *"Come on Caroline, you did not come all the way so you can safely sneak out again."*

I felt my body wanting to move. I felt the 'yes' again. Of course I can do it! Full of that yes I was on my way. The smile that started to lighten up my face only disappeared when I stood at the sinks outside of the Taman, where the sacred tobacco was being given.

My hands sweaty, my mouth dry, I said with a trembling voice, "Friends, I am going to take the tobacco too". Their encouragement overwhelmed me and tears started to flow. Feeling blessed to be supported by so many beautiful souls, I inhaled deeply then I took the syringe that was filled with the fluid and emptied it in my nose. My head felt as if my brain was lighting up. I could see clearer than before, the sweet smell of incense was more intense. With the energy rushing through my body I felt recharged. The music that was coming from the Taman sounded even more inviting than the day before. Full of excitement and curiosity I crossed the threshold.

Facing my fears, I broke free. No longer holding back, I danced, celebrating my existence. "I am here", I shouted joyfully, "I am here".

When Ratu one day, said I was going to bring laughter back home, I knew he was right.

The day before I was due to go home I went for a walk, guided by Margot, a French woman who had been at the ashram for a long time. While the sun caressed our skin, we bathed in the cool water of a spring that flowed from the mountain. Looking down on the wonderfully shaped green terraces, which contrasted with the blue sky above, I felt overjoyed. Carefully following the narrow pathways down the mountain, we headed back. As she turned to warn me to be careful I fell.

Falling and falling gave me time to wonder when I would hit the ground.
My spine cracked when I did. Everything went black. I thought I would never see my family again.

As I slowly returned to consciousness, a feeling of peace surrounded me.

Margot shouted my name to reassure me I was not alone. She found me in a crooked position, stuck between two walls of soil. When I was able to move my toes and arms a little, I was relieved that I wasn't paralysed. But my breath was labored and I tasted blood in my mouth. I waited as Margot went to get help. Soon a few men came with a stretcher to rescue me. My body could not stretch so they all generously took of jackets to support my back, and carried me into a little van they called an ambulance. Riding for hours on roads with more holes than asphalt, I could see the green of the trees flashing by.

Not having the means to examine me properly, I was put in a bed I could not adjust myself because the controls were placed on the outside. Non English-speaking nurses washed me, and tried to cheer me up. I felt too sick to bother about living, but I was somehow filled with gratitude. If not for Hans I would have given up. He urged the insurance company to take action. I was flown to Kuala Lumpur where soon after arrival my condition was revealed. I had broken my back in 8 places. Not fully grasping the extent of the situation I longed for Hans.

"So, be careful what you wish for, Caroline", he joked after our tears from feeling as if we met for the first time had dried. He was right. I had wanted to give up control; and now all I could do was just be. Hans helped me through the rehab process that started in bed first. His 'another 3, 2, 1' and 'yes, you did it' was what I needed to get ready to get out of bed and then, after a few weeks, to finally fly back home.

As I wore a bulky corset to support my back, my dear daughter lovingly called me 'ninja turtle'. Well, I certainly moved as slow as a turtle… if I moved at all. "But you are so cheerful, Caroline", was an often heard remark. Yes, I was cheerful, thankful even. Not only had I survived, I felt reborn. Sure, all the muscles in my back were cramped, walking to the bathroom and back left me exhausted, but I had a deep gratitude I had never experienced before. And as I had taught many of my clients: I don't need to identify with my body. I am far more than that.

I was tremendously intrigued by what had happened; surviving a ten meter fall had to tell me something. For years a woman named Fem, who channelled messages from the Masters of White Light, had coached me. The information has always been very helpful in bringing forth insights.

As soon as I was able to get into my car again I drove up to her for a private session. As I approached her apartment I started to feel excited, nervous even. Eager but also a bit scared to hear what those angels had to say. While Fem listened to the dictation she typed a letter. I sat in front of a monitor and saw the letters slowly turning into words, and the words turning into a profound message.

"You have been saved, dear lady. This always brings about a big change in existence, a rapid one even, as if time isn't that important anymore, and you will never, ever be the same as you were before. So what is this about? What power does this concern? Who are you and where are you going? What is it that wants to be expressed within you that such a drastic intervention was needed to 'bring you to your senses' and hopefully keep you there!?"

Your change, your rapid, renewal, is about coming to Source and to be strong enough to look through the mists. To, let's say, work with Truth, because you cannot stand your ground on your own. Don't think we are not respecting you, dear lady, but we want to be sincere with you and we know you can take a punch!

You are being found, you are being moved, you are performing an existence. And to be moved, both physically and emotionally, there is something greater than you. Love is not about putting two people together; it is about you unfolding so that you can see Love that has always been there. It is time to trust. The saying 'to see the Light' is not a random one. And we can assure you: when you do, you will find there is nothing more fulfilling."

Afterwards Fem and I sat there for a while in silence. Then she spoke. "Do you understand what they are talking about, Caroline?" I wasn't sure I did.

"About my higher Self?" I asked. She replied: "How about God?" And suddenly I understood, an understanding beyond words. Tears ran silently down my cheeks as I felt a shift I could not grasp. Before saying goodbye, she recommended some books and one of them was *A Course in Miracles*. The title had been mentioned to me several years ago. I wasn't ready then, but now I felt a calling so strong I decided to buy the book first thing the next day.

Reading the words, the beautiful language, although not always understanding intellectually, already brought even more peace. The thick book laid next to my bed, so every morning I could read a lesson and before going to sleep I did the same. It felt as if a loving family member was speaking to me. I became more aware of my opinions and how I still wanted to be in control, although not as strongly as before.

Doing the lessons time passed and suddenly one day, as I was driving my car, arguing with Hans, I was there and yet not there. A feeling of overflowing Love took possession and I quickly pulled over. Tears were pouring as I could only sob and say "Thank you, thank you." I was aware I sat in the car with Hans and simultaneously knew that all I saw in the world was from my own making. I knew that there was nothing out there, only me projecting. As I raised my hands in gratitude, tears kept on flowing. I saw Hans' loving eyes, also filled with tears, and heard him say "I don't know what is happening, but you are so beautiful."

The beauty of it all, to me, is that there is so much to be grateful for.

Yes, I have been in agony, both physically and emotionally. I can honestly say my life has been 'a bumpy ride'. The Balinese road is a beautiful metaphor, as is the fall. I cannot say it was an accident because I perceived it as a gift. All of it. And I learned that living is about "not my will, but Thine be done." A guidance so loving it often makes me cry with joy. That is what the miracle is all about, tuning into Love and knowing that everything is as it should be.

No need to judge.

No blame or shame.

As the angels had predicted, I have seen the light and can truly say there is nothing more fulfilling.

I thanked myself that finally I started to listen.

I wish you the same.

About the Author

Caroline Hoek is a transpersonal psychotherapist, coach, and trainer. While living in the Netherlands, she considers herself a global citizen and works with clients all over the world.

Caroline is the founder of Good Life Guidance. It is her deepest wish to accompany her clients on the path of personal and/or professional development. Rather than rigid protocols or models, it's her intuition and her 30+ years of experience that are her greatest strengths. Creating a safe, respectful and playful atmosphere, Caroline makes room for what needs to be addressed head on. There are no rules, only guidance for real transformation. Anchored in (self) trust she lets her clients discover their unique gifts and use them for inner and outer leadership.

To learn more you are invited to download a free e-book or listen to meditations at www.GoodLifeGuidance.com

Love as a Healing Power

Ninet Sommer

After 14 years of trying to conceive naturally, including 7 years of fertility treatments, my dear friend Christel was finally pregnant. At only three days post insemination, her blood test came back positive, which is almost unheard of. This soul was insistent on making its presence known.

During the first weeks of pregnancy, Christel was over the moon, envisioning herself becoming a mum, and starting a family with her dear husband. Each day felt like a miracle. She could sense the presence of her little girl from the start and spent her days in joyful conversation with her growing child.

In the twelfth week, they decided to go on a vacation to Thailand. Within the first days of their adventure, Christel started to bleed and developed a high fever, quickly becoming seriously ill and requiring hospitalization. The doctors could not identify what was going wrong, and while they offered her many types of medication, she refused, feeling unsure of the doctor's knowledge of the situation. After a few days she and her husband made the risky decision to sneak her out of the hospital and onto a plane back to Denmark, her fever hidden by the air conditioning of the plane.

Upon their return, they went straight to the hospital. An ultrasound revealed that Christel was carrying not only a baby girl, but a boy as well. The joyful news was quickly overshadowed by the doctor's terrible revelation. The baby boy's intestines were growing outside of his little body, and the heartbreaking reality was that his life would be short and full of medical complications.

Over the next few weeks, Christel and her husband agonized over how to proceed. They pursued multiple opinions, both from medical specialists and spiritual practitioners. It became clear that this child would have to endure countless operations from birth, unending pain, and would probably not survive past the first three years of his little life. After much heartbreak, they decided that sparing their child this short life of agony was the right choice. They made the hardest decision a parent will ever have to make, to end the life of their child. They knew this would put their daughter's life at risk as well, but they could not bear the alternative.

I visited her in the hospital at 15 weeks, and as soon as I saw her face, I knew something was wrong. She was broken with pain and desperation, fear and guilt, her body a dim reflection of her normally strong and assured self. She had lost her son and would not know how this choice would affect the life of her daughter.

In the face of these complications, the fertility hormones, the in utero procedure to end her son's life, and the presence of his lifeless body, the chances of her going to full term were unbearably low. These first 24 hours post surgery would indicate the prognosis for her daughter's life. As I sat with her in these devastating moments, crying, talking and holding one another, my heart was heavy with the sense of that little girl, lying in the safety of her beloved mother's belly, next to the body of her twin brother, and I could not bear that this would be her reality for the next five months. I felt an unwavering calling to help facilitate the journey of this little boy's soul back to its Source.

In that terrible moment, I could not say exactly what help was needed, but I knew for certain that I was meant to open myself and offer some healing to this family, and especially to those two beloved soul's within Christel's womb.

Since childhood, I always knew I had the ability to channel my love for the people around me into a force of healing energy. I also always felt clear that there was a spiritual force bigger than me and outside of me. I felt this force as light and love, rather than a specific religious concept or deity. I had always been fascinated by churches and sanctuaries, but I also had a knowing deep in my heart that guilt and shame were not in alignment with this higher power of love.

Each time throughout my life, when I have experienced the passing of someone close to me, I have felt the calling and ability to create a channel of love and light for them to ensure a safe and complete voyage back to their Source. I have never studied this, or really spoken to many about this ability, but I have always completed the process as it was revealed to me by this Higher Power, and I have always sensed the energetic exchange and gratitude from the souls I have partnered with in this work.

On that day, in the hospital room with dear Christel, I knew I had to try to support the soul of her baby boy on his journey back home, but I didn't know how to put this into words to explain to his devastated mum. I offered to pray for healing, and while Christel was not a believer in such things, she opened herself to the process and allowed me to share my gift.

Visitors were coming to support Christel, so I took my time in the hallway, knowing I needed to prepare my energy prior to engaging with this level of spiritual work.

I sat in the cramped corner of the hospital hallway, asking the universe for the peace and quiet which would be needed to connect with the energy of the spiritual healing.

Despite the weight of the oppressive hospital equipment, the devastation of the loss of their child and the pressure of the impending close of visiting hours, I focused first on filling the hospital room with beautiful and loving energy, envisioning a quiet but intense overflowing of love into every corner.

Once the loving space was created, and visitors had left, I could sense that Christel was ready to let go and surrender to a power greater than herself if needed. This was not in her nature, a typically strong and in control woman, however, out of her deep motherly love and the faith that grows out of desperation, she courageously offered her trust to me and surrendered to the unknown.

I stood next to her bed, placed my hands over her belly, and opened myself to the highest place in the universe of light and love, asking the universal power of healing to connect and enter my body and energy system. From that connected place, I flowed an abundance of the healing force of love deep into the bodies and spirits of Christel, the two souls cradled in her womb, and their father. I allowed the power of that love to expand, filling up every space in their bodies, every part of them, inside and out. The energy was like the purest magic ever, sparkling stars of crystal, radiance, tenderness, and love.

Holding that space of healing love, I saw a grey image. I knew that this was the soul of the little boy, and I could see him sitting on a swing, his face filled with confusion, sadness and sorrow.

I searched deep within myself for the power to connect with his little soul and we began to communicate without the need for words but in clear ideas nonetheless.

"Hello dear beautiful you," I said, as he looked to me with that deep confusion still in his eyes. "Where am I?," he asked.

"You are in a space between life and death, and this is the time to collect what you have already been given during your short life in this body. You are so loved, and you have brought so much love, joy and happiness into the life of your parents during this time."

As I continued, his gaze began to soften, the confusion dissipating from his little eyes. "In this incarnation, your body was very sick, too sick to stay with us. So dear one, you are free to go. Your sister is still in this body, and you need to say goodbye to her now, though this goodbye is not forever, you will meet again."

The energy around us was full of intense bright light and overflowing with love. The image shifted, and I saw him with his sister, holding hands in a field of flowers, deeply connected in their love. The purity and power of their connection was breathtaking in its beauty. They stayed there for a while, allowing their connection to heal their souls, and then I told them that it was time to say goodbye, it was time for him to pass on to the next phase of his journey.

Once more, I told him he was deeply loved, embracing him warmly with my heart, and whispered, "Thank you for coming."

I then asked for and created an opening to allow his soul to transfer from this life into the beyond. A channel of brilliant light opened and it was a sight of pure wonder, filled with shimmering angels, sparkling light, and expansive, alluring love, bigger and greater than life itself.

The boy and I exchanged one last glance, and his soul entered into and up the channel of light.

Next, I turned to his sister, she also needed guidance and support. She was still in the shock and distress of losing her brother, and I came to her to offer the calm reassurance of why he had needed to go, how very much her parents adored her, and how all of us were so looking forward to meeting her in person someday soon. I also told her that she would always have a special place in my heart because of what we had shared.

Once I was able to sense that she was calm and that her energy flow was back to a healthy place, I asked for healing of Christel's womb, and for the overall physical and mental healing of both Christel and her husband. I ended the healing by envisioning my beloved friend and the two babies as surrounded and held in a heavenly cloud of love.

"Thank you, thank you, thank you," I sent out from my heart to all my helpers, to the universe, to God, the guides, and the angels for this loving healing energy. Even though I did not fully understand or see all the help I had received, I knew that I had not done this work alone. I was only the instrument through which the love and healing was channeled.

As I opened my eyes, I looked down to see Christel, laying serenely on the hospital bed in the deepest sleep. I leaned over and kissed her forehead gently, leaving them in the warmth and healing energy of love.

The next morning, I received a teary call from Christel. At 3 o'clock in the morning, she had awoken to the feeling of blood between her legs and discovered the tiny, lifeless body of a fetus laying there. She gently lifted this little body into a cup and brought it desperately to the nurses. The doctor confirmed that it would likely be only a matter of time before she miscarried the other baby. Nobody checked which fetus had left the body. Christel was left in the powerless agony of waiting as she watched her dreams of motherhood slip away and out of her very body.

Hours ticked by laboriously with no changes. Finally, the doctor completed an ultrasound, and to their shock and unimaginable joy, there was a heartbeat! A miracle had occurred. The doctor's discovered that Christel's high fever and distress had been caused by her son's medical condition. Once his body left her womb, her temperature returned to normal and her health was restored.

Christel's daughter entered this world after only 5½ months in her mother's womb, weighing only 2lbs 5 oz. and requiring a 3 month stay in the hospital. After her delivery, Christel was given informational brochures about the medical complications and difficulties typical of premature babies. She read only the first page, and then decisively threw it in the garbage. She knew that was not her vision for her child! Christel and her husband never gave up, they drew power from their love for one other and for their child, and in this power the baby grew strong and healthy.

It has been 15 years since Mikka's birth. I recently has the honor of attending her Catholic confirmation ceremony. At the celebration afterwards, Mikka spoke to each person in attendance, and when she arrived at me, she shared simply and powerfully, "*You make me calm.*" These simple words confirmed to me that while we had never spoken about the healing session in the hospital, Mikka knew on some level, how my love had allowed the peace and calm that supported her in her yearning for life. With tears streaming down my face, I was filled with gratitude.

Both Christel and myself have always been aware of the deep connection between Mikka and me. We don't see each other very often anymore, but when we do, the love and safety we feel is immeasurable. She will truly always be one of the greatest miracles in my life.

Mikka is a beautiful, young woman, with a loving soul, so soft and gentle yet so very strong. Repeated times in life she has withdrawn from social contexts, as she does not understand why people consciously choose to be evil to each other instead of loving.

I sense that she still feels the absence of her soulmate, her dear twin brother. Despite the loving support of her family, within her there is a constant searching, a feeling of loneliness, and a doubting of her right to a place in this life.

Despite this doubt, Mikka continues with miraculous assurances that she is wanted, known, loved and supported on this earth. A pony named Jack came into her life, and as their connection and love blossomed for each other, an animal communicator told them that they shared a similar story. Christel had to investigate facts in this enlightenment and it got confirmed that Jack was rescued from a stable next to a dead pony. Like Mikka and her twin, Jack had come to know the loss of a dear soul, and through this shared experience, Jack and Mikka have become bonded in a deep and knowing love. An animal communicator taught her to communicate with Jack, which made their connection even deeper.

What are the chances this being a coincidence?

I believe it was planned in advance, as a loving and supportive gift from the universe.

As humans we have the tendency to feel alone and helpless, like we have to do everything ourselves. We are never alone. The universal help and support is all around us. Be open to it.

I believe in love as a divine resource that is available always to each of us.

I have been called to share this story, to be a signpost into understanding of the value of love as a healing power. My hope is that this story will become a great inspiration, and I ask you all to dare, to share your love and healing with the world.

About the Author

Ninet Sommer is a passionate heart healer, holistic health coach, family therapist and counselor, with a Bachelor's degree in pedagogy education based in Denmark. She meets the world with a smile and open heart. A sensitive fiery soul, with a deep respect for others. Her call is to serve the children, supporting them to stay centered and remember their special gift to the world.

Connected to the Mother-energy Ninet is here to share here love and healing with the world. She is passionate about her healing practices and holistic healthcare to help guide people into more balance in life. The proud mother of a 25 year old son, Ninet specializes in helping parents connect to their children from the heart, and hopes to inspire conscious heart-centered parents in supporting their children.

Ninet is currently writing a book with simple tools to support children to stay balanced in life – coming soon!

For more information visit www.ninetsommer.com
or send email to ninetsommer@gmail.com

Angel's Love Is Easy

Elspeth Kerr

I sat down to take a moment to pause…

To breathe in harmony with you…

To be with you…

To cherish this breath with you…

To cherish this moment with you…

To honor you…

I sat down to write this for you to understand where I've been, who I am right now and in every single moment as my destiny unfolds with divine love of life, as I walk home with you – hand in hand, with peace in my heart and joy in my soul celebrating the miracle of you!

Because you are here you matter…

I am a healer…

I serve…

I live…

I am a teacher…

I am a student…

I celebrate the wonderful miracle of life as best I can…

After many lessons, what I know for sure, is we will never have peace until we find peace within. Finding this precious space of peace inside of us is where true healing begins to unfold and manifest.

My given name is Elspeth Kerr but I can assure you I am so much more than just my name. I can also assure you, that your soul, like mine, is also so much more than just your name!

Namaste to you, dear soul.

I honor the miracle of you because I know you honor the miracle of me too.

Letting go of our name, our restrictions, our limiting beliefs, our "boxes" or as some like to say "the lines that divide us" from one another, is paramount. This allows us to fully embrace and truly understand and integrate the light and the beauty of the divine miracle of oneself! The miracle of the "light being" that we all are.

Our original soul…

Our original light…

Our original spirit…

My only job and intention is to honor the miracle of YOU! The miracle that your heart and soul is… that you *exist!*

The timelessness of our wonderful Universe is truly amazing.

I must begin by honoring my mother – I was literally born from "love" as "Love" was my mother's middle name.

My mother and father chose my name Elspeth, which is a feminine name and the Scottish equivalent of Elizabeth. It means, "Consecrated by God." I say this with absolute humility. I am very grateful to my parents, now in heaven, for giving me this precious name that allowed me to learn to love myself enough to share my story with you and with those who cross my path.

We are all magical and miraculous divine sparks of God's brilliant, vibrant, holy and unending love. The love that literally put all that we see and know together as one.

What I feel is that love itself is the energy, vibration, and frequency that holds us all together. Love is the glue of the Universe and of God – Joy is the gift that comes from this love once realized.

After all these miles I've travelled – magic and miracles are as real as the sun and the moon, the earth and the sky, and as exciting and as inspiring as all the stars combined.

What a miracle it is to be right here – right now – with you – as you read these words holding this wonderful, blessed, miraculous book in your magical hearts and souls. What a blessing for you and I to meet with almost 8 billion people on earth. I know there is no mistake in you holding this magical book. It was destined to be – and the flow of life-force-energy and consciousness aligned this moment together with pure Divine Love.

In the early years of my own life I didn't fully understand this concept. Long, long ago, when I was a small child, I remember telling those around me that I had friends that nobody could see with their physical eyes. My spirit friends were as real to me then as they are today, and the beauty of it is, I have no interest in proving any of it anymore to anyone. Instead I just "know" and let it be as it is with pure joy in my heart and soul.

Growing up on a farm in Scotland allowed me to understand and know that the planet is magical. I have so much to thank my dad for, as he was an amazing teacher to me and shared with me the knowledge and wisdom that I share every single day.

I want to help others understand the divine beauty within. I do this by being a Soul to Soul reader of the Heart, a counselor, a Podiatrist, a Reiki Master, a Meditation Teacher/Practitioner, a Hypnotherapist, a Reflexologist, a Massage Therapist, a NLP and EFT Practitioner, and a Colour and Crystal Therapist. I am also a medium and I help and support other people who are changing the world…..people who are enriching this planet with divine love and goodness. I love helping people to thrive and succeed!

I have taught Reiki and meditation for 22 years and I feel very blessed by those souls who have crossed my path on our shared journey of life to this special space we are now in. And what a ride it has been…from being an active extrovert to being bedridden with no energy when I was diagnosed with an ailment that literally stole my energy and made it virtually impossible to stay awake.

At that time in my life, I was more tired waking up after a full night's sleep than if I had run a marathon! I had no energy whatsoever. It was a terrible time when I lost friends as many people didn't understand my health condition or know why I was always exhausted.

I had Myalgic Encephalomyelitis, M.E., a neurological disease. *My* = muscle. *Algic* = pain. *Encephalo* = brain. *Mye* = spinal cord.

M.E. was and still is at times, a very frustrating struggle, but it is one that I understand has provided compassion and grace on a level that is truly extraordinary. I also know that each day I get better and better and my energy comes back more and more as I bring the divine love within me to life with intention. I move from a space of "Doing" to a space of "Being." I let go of my limitation and simply take each moment as it unfolds with JOY in my heart for being alive and able to help others as best I can, when I can.

To compensate for my lack of energy there was even a time that my family and I decided to purchase a motorhome so I could go away and be able to sleep and rest when necessary while on vacation. There were times back then that it was absolutely impossible for me to walk 3 steps, let alone be on vacation for weeks at a time. The motorhome allowed me to make memories with my daughter and husband; and it created some of our most cherished times together as a family. All those years ago we lived in Scotland and since that time my body guided me to move to Paphos Cyprus. I wanted to be able to enjoy the sun and be near the wonderful warm ocean waters with the holy, healing, spiritual vibration and energy of Aphrodite – The Greek Goddess of Life, Love, and Beauty.

It took years to get better – even now I have days where I am wiped out. Within me I know and understand that it's due to my chosen lessons of service this lifetime: unconsciously giving energy to Mother Earth so she can awaken to new energies we have on our planet. I help her by reminding others of the importance of taking care of Gaia with all of our love and at the same time taking care of our own well being.

Music also played a vital part in my healing. At one point when I couldn't read or even watch T.V. as it was too exhausting. I would lie in bed and listen to music. The soft, gentle tones helped me tremendously to feel the vibrations of the healing frequencies of pure love in the musician's heart and soul streaming through me.

More recently, I met a sound healing musician named Paul Luftenegger who has changed my life, both personally and also with my clients and students. Paul's incredible energy-work has helped change people's lives all around the world. He calls his music, "conscious healing music." Paul writes his magical music to inspire and promote global love and kindness from within the listener. His peaceful, positive music is from source/God and is infused with amazing healing frequencies.

Playing Paul's music in my healing room every day keeps the vibration of the room at a high-level so when clients enter they feel peaceful frequencies and it also heals and balances me in the process. As a healer and intuitive, I know we will have huge breakthroughs as we more fully understand the importance of sound, frequency, and vibrations.

Here are the links to Paul Luftenegger's website where you can find out more about his healing music for those who wish to heal on a deep heart/soul level: www.beekindness.com or

www.paulluftenegger.com

I've healed from having M.E. I had cancer, and was given a diagnosis of 6 to 9 months to live by my doctor. I also healed from that. I've healed from two near death experiences. Miracle after miracle I am still here, alive and writing you this message! My intention is to spread love and kindness daily.

Souls are drawn to me as I understand the space they are in and they always leave my healing-space feeling lighter and transformed. Their heart, their soul, and their spirit is lifted up and empowered by the miracle within them. This important connection with the Universe and with God is paramount to understand because it is what recharges our inner light.

We all share the same sun; a star that magically lights up the world so that life can exist for all of us to share together. Yet it never expects a single thing in return for shining its brilliant warmth to sustain our lives.

We are all surrounded by so many miracles; we just need to be open enough to see them and realize they are right before us in every single moment. It is these moments that make our life whole and magical.

The key to JOY itself is inside of each of us waiting patiently to be discovered. The only way to truly find our BLISS is to go within!

The question we must ask, is where is life truly experienced? On the inside or the outside?

If you gently throw a ball to someone – where does the experience really exist for the person catching the ball? Is the experience on the inside or the outside of the catcher? The reality is, the sensations and the soul experience takes place inside, the outside is only the stimulus.

I like to look at the body as a vehicle; the driver of the body is the heart, soul, and spirit working together in perfect harmony. Consciously making choices that are positive, loving and kind for us and others create a positive, loving life.

It is your heart, soul, and spirit that has this master key and with it, the ability to open all the good blessings possible for you in this lifetime, from the inside out. The sacred garden and the divine inner-technology is within each and every single one of us. This same divine design is in all of us. If we can all help one another to remember this we will all thrive with a love like never before.

Only you can open your doors with this master key and it takes this understanding to fully embrace the miracles waiting for you on the journey of your lifetime, which is your destiny, divinely designed uniquely just for you. Your path and your journey

When Peace Surpasses Understanding

is yours alone and it is as unique as your fingerprints and as genuine sacred as your individual cells.

I've learned over the years that life teaches us what we need to know through our experiences to help us become all that we can be for the greatest good of humanity. I believe that we are each a gift from the Universe to each other. Our job is to remember the gift we came to bring to life and to share our gifts openly.

The reality is – it is the life that we live that helps the world become all that it can be – the world in perfect harmony! We cannot do this alone. Not you. Not me. No one. This is a shared journey – a journey of coming together as one love.

We must take better care of this precious jewel of a planet. The home that we all share is a living and breathing treasure to cherish and protect. Gaia's soul is so beautiful…she is as alive as you are. She is aware of your soul at all times and understands the beauty and miracle of you. Her only request is for you to take care of her as she has taken care of you. We are all made from Gaia's vibrations; her earth and soil mixed with sunlight and water, and of course energized and infused by source/God.

I hope my story has positively touched your heart and soul. I have always done my best to be an inspiration. What I deeply believe most is that Love and Joy are what the world needs. So expand the love and feel the joy from the inside out – then you'll own your magic and be the miracle that you are with full power. Let the miracles and magic flow from within you and watch them surround you and all of life more and more!

Last, I thank God and all the Angels, those in Spirit along with all souls who have helped on my earth-journey!

The Healing Smile

I'm lying here, my weighty body upon my bed
I see your smile as you walk into my lonely space
Your smiling face radiating down on me
I feel your love penetrating through and through
You'll never know how wonderful this feels to me
It's allowing my heart to melt and open more
Our energies now mixing and melding together
You've brought me hope of tomorrow
You've shown me the way by your smile
By opening your heart and allowing the Love to flow
You gently took my hand in yours
 The warmth, the touch, such a refreshing breath
 I drink it all in now, close my eyes and drift off into another
world of dreams and sleep
Thank you for coming
For being there
For sharing what your hearts filled with
Thank you for your love, your touch
And above all I thank you for your
Healing Smile

   SMILE = Start My Internal Love Engine

Om Shanti
Xx Elspeth

About the Author

My name is Elspeth Kerr, I was born in Scotland and moved to Cyprus to follow my bliss. I am married and a mum of one daughter whom I love deeply. I am a soul reader of the heart and I teach Reiki and self-empowerment. I use my knowledge to help souls shine with joy from the inside out. I help the soul smile and beam its divine radiant light through direct connection that the soul has to source. I remind my clients to own their smile, which starts their internal 'Love Engine.'

I look to nature for my answers spending my days supporting Gaia. I liberate the heart and soul through the original nature of Spirit. My healing space is a safe place to release. I offer the world my services via Skype and in-person-sessions to find the magic and miracle within.

Connect with Elspeth:
www.facebook.com/elspeth.kerr.3
Email: Elspethkerr2508@gmail.com

Visit Soundcloud.com to find my Healing Steps of Colour Transformation audio.

The Sixth Sense

Understanding Our Inner Divine Sacred Technology

Paul Luftenegger

Our Soul's Holy Worth

I am a musical medium, clairaudient, and an Ascension Guide with God's holy love and grace.

I can safely say, with absolute certainty, that my whole life is miraculous and magical because of God's holy love that nurtured and cared for me enough to share what I know and pass the metaphorical baton to you…

I was called by God to do this sacred, holy work in 2011, much like how many priests and ministers explain receiving their sacred call from God to the church or pulpit. My call from God came from countless magical miraculous moments with God loving me whole again after my father's tragic suicide which happened on March 6th of 2011.

In many ways the old me died that day and the new hybrid, the highest version of my best self began to bloom its eternal, sacred, infinite, holy, magical blooms.

Seeing someone kill themselves and abandoning their life is a stain in the fabric of the heart and soul that is very hard to clean and heal because it hurts terribly. I wish this pain and trauma on no one. I have complete empathy and compassion for anyone suffering here on planet earth and I know that many are in dire pain, often trapped in the pain of shame.

What I know for sure is that pain is totally and completely relative. Sadly, hurt people hurt other people in response to their own suffering instead of transcending their suffering with and through the divine love of God.

We are in a time of evolutionary growth. We all must grow up spiritually by taking hold of our own reigns or better yet our own steering wheels and becoming completely responsible for the energy we create. We are in a whole new planetary age on this new earth that has been predicted by sages, saints, and divine masters for many thousands of years.

The great part is we are all so very blessed to be on earth right now, we're here with some of the most incredible beautiful brilliant timeless souls that have ever been – and if you are reading this you are likely one of them! This is not a solo mission. We are all here together to put away competition and conflict and integrate the peacefulness of holy sacred oneness.

One Earth. One Crew. One Spaceship.

When you leave earth and look back it is one world.

We must all remember we are on the same team; the same crew!

This is the holy nature and the holy grail of this new Ascended earth in the 5th dimension and beyond. The earth has already Ascended. We are the ones catching up to her wonderful vibrational frequencies to help each of us with our own personal Ascension. To Ascend ultimately means becoming one's best and highest self in manifest form right here on Earth.

We are living in a new age where co+creation is fully becoming manifest. No more lines of separation that divide us from our loving holy source (God), nor from one another. We are all sacred divine holy brothers and sisters and we must all become the captain and master of our own fate with God's will fused with our own. The only way this is truly possible is with the sacred truth of the immortal soul in unity with the cosmos.

The Day My Father Died by Suicide

The day my father died I realized I was no longer strong enough or big enough to do this life alone. I fell into a deep, dark space where I thought I was dying. On bended knees before God, in front of the bathroom mirror, where I could no longer bear the pain or breathe that morning, while pulling my hair out of my head, I prayed to God to save me and to heal me. I thought I was dying of a broken heart and a broken soul.

I remember looking deep into my eyes that morning, praying into my pupils, asking God to help me. To my surprise, God came and filled my heart with compassionate, pure, holy, divine love and light, restoring a sacred understanding of who I truly am.

Writing this for you makes me cry because for the first time, on March 6th 2011, I realized that I was what's inside of me, and not what is outside of me. That I am my heart and that I am my soul with the Holy Spirit, and that the outside world is separate from me. I became sovereign with God's pure love for me that day and each day since.

For years God has held me in his loving kind arms every single day when I thought I could no longer survive on this earth.

My pain was trumped by God's will to love me until I could walk, talk, and sing again. I was liberated by God's love to stop being afraid, to be the divine loving light, the sacred soul and the pure heart with the Holy Spirit that I am — remembering my original pure light and my divine pure essence with God always there to help me thrive.

God's message to me soon after my father's suicide was that I would write music to help the world forever. I remember thinking that God was absolutely, totally nuts and had lost it, knowing that I was not a singer and certainly not a public person that could perform whatsoever!

I remember trying to tell God that he had got it all wrong — that I was the wrong person for this mission and that I was not big enough, strong enough, smart enough, or good enough to write the music that God was asking me to produce and create.

I remember God just looking at me and smiling with pure love — saying absolutely nothing. The silence was deafening so I began to play and play and play and then sing and sing and sing opening up my heart and my soul to God. I remember God coming through the core of all that I am with a light of pure love more beautiful than anything I have ever experienced before. I was astonished by the miracles every single time and in fact I still am.

I remember every single miracle that took place at the piano. Each song is a message for the world from God.

With Humility and Gratitude

Here we are 8 years later… my music from 6 conscious albums with two singles have been used at the United Nations 3 times in New York City.

My music has been used to honour the incredible life work of Louise Hay in front of 2000 people, which was live-streamed all around the world on Louise Hay's last birthday.

My music has been used by countless teachers and by students from all around the world – helping hearts and souls understand their divine, sacred worth and their pure, gorgeous inner beauty.

I have received letters from people in so many countries thanking me for helping their heart and their soul to light up with more divine love.

I have met princes, New York Times best selling authors, and many famous spiritual teachers. I even have a recorded telephone message from Oprah Winfrey that was sent to me by her neighbour in Hawaii thanking this neighbour for gifting her my CDs.

My music was even contracted by the hit show *"So You Think You Can Dance"* and privately performed by two of their amazing Choreographers as a surprise for Louise Hay's birthday!

I have been invited to India, the USA, Denmark, Norway, Iceland, Sweden, Switzerland, Germany, England, Holland, Australia, Spain, Belgium, France, Vietnam, Singapore, Malaysia, Japan, China, Cambodia, the Philippines, Cyprus, and so many more countries as a result of my contribution to help humanity with conscious, kind, loving, positive, healing music.

This is what makes me cry with gratitude because God knew exactly what I would do and all that I needed when I had no idea whatsoever. I share this with humility because I thought I wasn't good enough to do any of this. I now realize that the only way to fully Ascend with God is to surrender to God's pure holy love and to bring that pure holy love into full alignment from the inside out – to find the flow that is destined for oneself.

My Own Ascension

My own Ascension process began the day I saw my father hanging by a rope from a steel beam in our family home. That sad day in March, where my heart broke into billions of pieces, I surrendered to God from the inside out and my whole world and universe shifted on a dime.

Was it easy? No. Would I change anything? No.

It isn't about me and my single will. What we all must come to understand is that though we all have free will there is a master plan. This plan includes our free will coupled with God's divine will. God's divine will shall always be done no matter what because God's divine love and divine light has already won the whole game of life.

That morning, while praying to God to help me, in my darkest moment, God came and answered every single prayer that day and each and every single day since. It is as if my Ascension and healing with God is fully integrated – much like how I was before I came to earth as Paul Luftenegger. Ultimately, I remembered that I was always with God's pure divine holy love and integrated this intimacy into my whole light body allowing my cup to run-neth over with God's divine holy nectar in the plasma of every particle that is me; the whole being that makes me all that I am. I am now in full form with my pure essence in divine flow!

My Work

I work and specialize in divine frequencies. My sacred mission on Earth is to help souls that are ready to feel their divine worth, clearly understanding a sacred inner technology by cleaning up some of the confusion and bringing the plasma lightbody into alignment and into a fuller bloom of understanding. Ultimately, the aim is to help all beings of love to thrive with divine love from the inside out.

I work for and with God in unity to help serve hearts and souls to understand the divine frequencies required to Ascend. This is where the heart and soul integrates together in an inner, peaceful process allowing the divine universal mind to come online with more clarity and understanding. I guess you could say I help my clients understand the process of how to reach God with much more certainty. The reality is that it begins with self-love, self kindness and understanding one's divine sacred worth from the inside out.

I have given many private sessions over the years, tapping in and going through what I call an "Ascension Reading" session. The messages that come through in these readings are truly awe-some! They are such a beautiful shared process and holy space with our teams from beyond the veils, who include our departed loved ones and our own spiritual guides. This includes angels, archangels, and Ascension Masters from all over the cosmos!

Before we begin to really dive into Ascension we must understand that the frequencies of heaven are right here, right now on Earth. Much like a tuning fork that helps the piano tuner tune the piano with frequencies, my job is quite similar, I help people tune into God's divine holy love.

We must all tune into God's pure loving frequencies by raising our own frequencies to love, which means letting go of the 'pain body' and rising up to God's divine holy loving frequency, which is paradise often known as heaven.

The challenge is that our own earth experiences are often dense. Sadly, many get stuck in the pain, misery, and low vibrational victim vibrations that block the process of integration. I often call these pains and traumas 'veils' or 'masks'.

The only way to God and to integrate God's inner technology is with and through pure divine holy love frequencies and vibrations. The only place to really do this is inside the heart and inside the soul.

It all begins with the way you see the Universe and the choice is so simple. You have a choice in each moment to see the Universe as hostile or loving.

The only way to Ascension is to choose to believe that we live in a loving, kind, conscious, beautiful, heavenly Universe!

The Holy Trinity: The Sacred Heart, The Eternal Soul, The Divine Mind

The sacred heart, the eternal soul, and divine mind must become one unit of inner peace connected to an inner loving river of source (God).

When this magical miraculous process fully integrates and blooms one Ascends, lighting up the aura from within oneself, making the plasma lightbody inside shine with pure holiness and reverence for the miracle that life truly is.

In a nutshell — this is what Ascension is all about — the integration of these 3 inner sacred technologies working together with God to form the 6th sense.

The first clear understanding we must all come to terms with is that the soul is a piece and a part of God's pure, infinite, holy, divine love. We must also understand that the soul drives and powers the body much like a car. Without the soul in the body and in the driver's seat with consciousness and control over all the operating systems, there is no life force energy and no driver to drive the car. This is proven simply by the physical death of the body itself — no soul, no life in the body.

Sadly, many have forgotten that the soul is a piece and a part of God. I say this with humility because I too have forgotten this fact at times. In our forgetfulness we may react to others in ways that are brutal and often cruel. This is what makes me cry at times because so few of us remember that we are all from the same divine pure loving, sacred, infinite source (God).

Often with veils of programs and masks of unworthiness placed upon us that cover our soul with layers and layers of densities and sludge – the pains and traumas the soul finds hard to let go of – which makes the soul's light dim – shackled from freedom and love and ultimately where the soul comes from (source). I see many souls in shackles on earth and I have learned that having compassion for those that are hurting is one of the greatest gifts and tools we have to help this world – not always easy but very important.

The heart is such a vital sacred part where Ascension must always begin. There is no other way. So many people are in jobs that they hate, making money to pay for things that they loathe buying and detesting the whole system of work. I say this because this was the old me. I used to be this person. I used to work chasing the metaphorical carrot that was dangling from a fixed position that I could never reach or attain. Somewhat like a dog chasing its tail, never catching what it seeks.

The truth is it is up to the soul to find its way home to source (God). The enlightened spiritual path and journey is available to each and every single one of us and God is patiently waiting for all souls to awaken to this beautiful truth. It is inevitable as every single soul will hear a knock at the door to come into this divine sacred awareness at some point of the journey and cycle of life. Each soul is a part of God's love and light (source), much like water, the soul must always return to its source.

Ascension with the 6th sense is choosing to do this consciously right here right now before the physical death. The beauty is that telepathy and the sixth sense come from the heart's vibrational frequency in tune with God's pure love, with the soul working together with life happening for us and not to us.

About the Author

Paul Luftenegger is an international multi-award winning singer, songwriter, and composer. Paul writes conscious music to inspire and promote global love and kindness from within. Paul's focus is nurturing self worth within the listener. He has performed for the United Nations 3 times and his music has been used to honour icons like Louise Hay.

Paul serves the "Starkey Hearing Foundation" helping to give free hearing aids to those in need around the world. His song Diamond Light won the 'Honourable Mention Award' from the USA International Songwriting Competition in 2013 and the album of the same name, the Top 10 Award by the London Free Press. Paul's music is used in classrooms worldwide to help children understand the importance of self-love and self kindness. Paul tours with his music and provides healing workshops around the globe – singing, speaking, and teaching.

Paul Luftenegger's Albums & Singles:

Albums:
1. Beautiful World / Blessings From Above (2011)
2. Worthy (2012)
3. Diamond Light (2013)
4. Love Expanding Love (2014)
5. The Miracle of You (2015)
6. Faith (2017)

Singles:
1. I Believe in You (2016)
2. Northstar, (2016)

Connect with Paul at www.beekindness.com
Email: info@paulluftenegger.com
www.facebook.com/luftenegger/
www.twitter.com/luftenegger
www.instagram.com/paulandcori

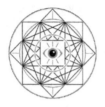

Part 3
Visions Beyond The Physical Realm

For as long as I can remember, I've seen visions of things that could happen, were about to happen, or had just happened. During my childhood, I had precognitive dreams that I found fascinating — and frustrating. It was kind of cool to see things before they happened, but when I started to get clear pictures or images of things that were scary, just as they were happening, I wondered what good it was.

Many of us have the natural ability to get information or feel the present, past or future physical and emotional states of others — including animals and spirits — without the use of the normal five senses. This ability now informs nearly every area of my life.

With study and insight, many of my friends and colleagues have realized that being an empathic visionary is indeed a gift, not a curse. In fact, as one comes to accept that these qualities make us who we are we become more comfortable talking about them with other people instead of hiding them. In my case, it has opened the door to being able to use these gifts for the benefits of my patients, clients, friends and my family.

Several people with various gifts of high sensory processing, extra sensory perception, the ability to speak to and hear spirits from other dimensions are quite 'ordinary' people, just with extraordinary talents.

The human body is endowed with sensory receivers which enable us to perceive information from the non-physical realm. The neurological networks in our brains, hearts, and intestines provide us with rich antennae to receive and emit electrical impulses and data, to and from our surroundings.

Our brains are also hardwired to know God — experientially — all of us can meet the Divine without crossing over to the other side nor being near death. So, as you read this book, know that many of the mind-blowing experiences that seem out of this world are accessible to you and me, too! The use breath work, guided meditations, brainwave entrainment devices and QiGong May help to quiet the mind, create altered states of consciousness and attune to frequencies of love and compassion. Getting in touch with fields of creativity and love also make it easy to see beyond this physical world.

But life itself has a way of opening up these capacities for us, often through painful crashes, near death experiences, or when we finally throw our hands up in despair. Sometimes just surrendering in a moment of need or fully relaxing into a moment of confusion can lead to out of body, visionary, mind expanding experiences.

What I've come to understand is that surrender is not actually an act of weakness or admitting defeat. Letting go of your need to control everything while engaged in prayer and meditation, laying down your sword in battle, or calling out to the universe for help, can be the very acts of opening and allowing which call forth new strength and powers.

Letting go through surrender can provide you with clear vision to see through obstacles or at least shed light on how to bypass or overcome them. Surrender offers you an initiation into a new level of existence, fortified with mystical powers you didn't know were available to you.

The stories in Part 3 demonstrate a little of that sort of magic.

How I Learned to "Be Love"

Diane L. Haworth

I've been through a lot in my life. I had chronically ill parents, was cheated on by my first love, had a dangerous first pregnancy, which resulted in my daughter being born 12 weeks early weighing only two pounds. I was in a long-term abusive relationship, had lingering weight and health issues, broken bones, car accidents, financial challenges…yep, I've lived a full life.

But I figured it out. After years of attending a traditional church, listening to Oprah, reading every spiritual and metaphysical book I could get my hands on and learning to meditate…I got it. I gradually realized that my journey was to pursue a spiritual path focused on divine love.

So, I got busy. I quit my job, started my own business and got to work. I spoke about love. I wrote about love. I did YouTube videos on love. I attended workshops on love. I read books on love. I was busy with the business of love while trying to understand how to be the presence of love for myself, my family, my clients, and the world.

Why?

I knew that each of us, at our core, are the essence of divine love and when we can learn to live from that place, our lives change. We're happier, healthier, more at peace. Life is more FUN. That's what it means to live love.

While I made great progress over the years, my process was still missing a few details. I wanted to live love but how the heck do I do that? To find the answer, I meditated daily and kept up with my love research. One day I realized wearing T-shirts with LOVE beautifully embroidered on the front simply wasn't enough. I knew there must be more to this love thing.

I knew, in the depth of my being, that *love* was the key to a genuinely happy, healthy, productive, passion filled life. I just wasn't sure where that pesky key was hiding! So I kept looking.

Then one day, it happened. Love found me in the most unexpected way.

The Workshop Experience

I was attending a weekend workshop by my mentor, Dr. Robert Holden, as part of a Hay House event in Toronto. Hay House has published many of the self-help, inspirational books that helped me *literally* transform my life and their events offer a unique opportunity to meet and learn from the world's top spiritual and metaphysical experts. I was excited to see my teacher, deepen into my understanding of love, and meet new like minded people. Robert is a student of *A Course in Miracles*, and his teachings have given me a solid foundation in the subject of divine love. He uses the term "Love" where others use "God," "Universe" or "Source." Right up my alley!

I had attended this workshop before so, I must admit, my expectations were more focused on a fun weekend away than on experiencing a life-changing event.

I arrived early for the two-day "Coach Camp," and sat next to a friend, prepared to enjoy the teachings to come. During one of the class segments dedicated to Robert's work detailed in his book *Loveability*, we were told that "love IS the answer and Love HAS the answers." We were reminded that Love is intelligent, truly our "ultimate coach" and we need only ask to be guided on any life issue. Then it was time for a quick class exercise.

We were invited to imagine we were having a "coaching session" with Love. As I remember it, we were to imagine we were standing on a "foundation of love" and were to draw that energy into our hearts. We were to close our eyes, go inside, and connect to the intelligent Love within. We were to then silently ask, *"Love, what would you most like me to know today?"* and listen for the response. Since I'd done this exercise before, I wasn't expecting the fireworks that followed.

As I prepared for the exercise, I imagined myself totally supported by love as I breathed deeply and silently asked the question, *"Love, what do you most want me to know today?"*

In my mind I heard, *"Be Love."* And in the span of a single heartbeat I saw a cascade of images, like I was seeing a series of stills from an old movie film reel. I saw myself walking up the three steps to my daughter's front porch. As an observer, I saw myself looking through the glass front door to see my then fifteen-month-old grandson, Emory. I could SEE the energy of love bouncing back and forth between us as his little face broke into a wide grin when he recognized his GiGi, his name for me.

I then heard distinctly, *"Greet everyone with an open heart, without an agenda."*

In a flash I was inside the house, looking at my beloved Emory. But I wasn't seeing his angelic face and toddler body. I was looking THROUGH him into a beautiful effervescent light at his core that I recognized as his soul. I then heard, *"See the divine essence in everyone."*

Before I knew it, Emory and I were alone in the living room, playing with his blocks. He awkwardly tossed one to me, as a toddler does, hitting me on the cheek. Immediately I felt only compassion, understanding he hadn't yet honed his throwing skills. He meant no harm. Again, the inner knowing came through loud and clear, *"Forgive quickly, completely, unconditionally. He's a baby. He's just learning."*

Suddenly I was in a dark space and could see only the outline of a door, which slowly cracked open. A bright, yellow light teaming with vibrant, joyful energy began to stream out. Just that small amount overwhelmed me with a feeling of bliss I could barely comprehend. Tears started to stream down my cheeks as I heard, *"You're all trying to get back here. You don't understand. You're already there. You never left. You just have to remember."* I realized the love I felt for Emory is but a tiny fraction of the love that is in the light of the ALL. It was awe inspiring. My mind could barely comprehend what had just occurred. It was beyond anything I can put into words. I sat speechless as the tears continue to flow.

And then it was over.

I got through the rest of the day in a bit of a daze and later met friends for dinner. Back to my "normal" self, the events of the day seemed distant by the time I went back to my hotel room and called my husband Joe, to say goodnight.

An Unspeakable Horror

"Did you have a good day?" He asked his usual question, but I sensed something was off. His voice sounded hesitant, softer than normal. Then he told me.

The unthinkable had happened.

Someone we knew had killed their only child, then taken their own life leaving a devastated ex-spouse, a grieving family, and shocked community. My mind reeled in disbelief.

For the second time that day, I found it hard to speak. My husband tried to comfort me, but he was dealing with his own sadness. I hung up the phone, alone with my thoughts.

I could understand the levels of depression and hopelessness that could lead someone to consider taking their own life. I've been there. But their child's? Their own flesh and blood? How could a loving parent deliberately take the life of their child? I couldn't get my mind around it.

It was unspeakable.

As I struggled to sleep, I imagined the last moments experienced by that precious child. The flash of understanding right before the end came…and the tortured thoughts of the parent who thought this was their only option.

Around 3am, I sat up in bed and said aloud to God, *"You have to show me how to be with this. I know I can't do anything, but how am I supposed to BE with this?"*

I heard the answer loud and clear:

"Be love.
Greet everyone with an open heart, without an agenda.
See the divine essence in everyone.
Forgive quickly, completely, unconditionally.
You're all just babies. You're all just learning."

I sat in bed, dumbfounded, stunned by the awareness that was growing steadily within me.

Earlier in the spring, I started a new routine at the beginning and end of my day. For years, I'd mentally listed each person, situation, and thing I was grateful for in the proceeding hours and had added recently from the prayer of St. Francis to my process. "Make me an instrument of your divine peace. Show me how to serve."

"Was this in response to my prayer?" I wondered, as I finally drifted off to sleep.

The Truth Unveiled in Silence

I woke the next morning and discovered I had totally lost my voice. I could speak only in the slightest whisper. I tried clearing my throat, gargling, coughing. Nothing worked. I had coughed a little the day before during class but hadn't felt sick. This was totally unexpected! My throat felt raw. I was tired and in pain. But I still had to finish my last day of the workshop.

And so, my time in silence began.

I attended the workshop, unable to participate in exercises except with faint whispers, hand gestures, and quick notes. Strangers offered lozenges, energy healing, and hot drinks. Their concern and loving care got me through the rest of the class.

All the while, I was thinking about my grieving friend, the family that was forever changed, and the instructions I had been gifted the previous day on how to "be love." It was hard to think of anything else. I remember feeling so blessed to be processing it all in the cocoon of love that Robert and the group had created.

I left for home the next day and arrived with a fever. By now I could only communicate by text as my voice was too weak to be heard over the phone. My husband took me to the doctor, and I was diagnosed with a nasty "bug" that can affect airline travelers and was prescribed strong antibiotics with steroids. The doctor then ordered me to be on "total voice rest" for seven full days.

Seven Days Without Talking

Those seven days became one of the most significant gifts of my life. Forced to go inside to process my pain, I kept a small journal to document my thoughts and feelings. I couldn't discuss what had happened with anyone, couldn't keep repeating my dramatic story to others, or hear myself relive the experience. My experience had indeed become "unspeakable."

A profound understanding began to emerge. Although surrounded by others, I felt utterly alone. Because I felt like no one understood or "heard" me, I could better understand the loneliness and despair felt by others.

"This is what it feels like to feel separate from the light," I thought, remembering the vibrant celestial light I saw emerge from the crack in the door in my vision.

That realization was like a physical blow to my heart. I *felt* it. Who could live this way? I saw the image of the parent who had taken their life flash before me. I saw their face twisted in the kind of anguish that makes the body writhe in pain. For a split second, I felt their agony before the final event. Suddenly, in my mind's eye I saw a waterfall of images...the elderly, refugees, prisoners, struggling parents, children in abusive situations, addicts, the terminally ill. I realized there are millions of people who feel separated from the light of Love every minute of the day.

I realized each of these haunted images were children of God, just like I was and those I love. Suddenly they seemed more real. A part of me. Since I believe that we are all part of the energy of an intelligent Universe, of course they are each part of me. Part of each of us. But what was I to do with this new understanding?

Then I understood. It's time to share the story.

"Love, what would you most have me know today?"

"Be love. Greet everyone with an open heart, without an agenda. See the divine essence in everyone. Forgive quickly, completely, unconditionally."

Putting Love into Practice

I am fully committed to doing my best to "be love" day to day, moment by moment, as best I can. I've spent time in meditation asking for additional guidance on exactly how to do that and the process continues to evolve. I've been given some suggestions that might benefit anyone who wants to live a life of love so they can experience more happiness, peace, and purpose each day.

Greet everyone with an open heart, without an agenda

- Start with yourself. Take a breath, smile and greet yourself in the mirror each morning. No comments, no judging. Just a heartfelt greeting and sincere wish for a lovely day.

- Remind yourself to smile at everyone and everything. Not just your family but also the postman, the person sitting next to you in traffic, the neighbor's dog. Greet everyone with love and without any agenda or expectations.

- Ask Love for guidance when you need it. "Love, you know I'm not crazy about my boss. How do I greet him with an open heart?" Listen, and feel, for your answer.

See the divine essence in everyone

- Again, ask to see this in yourself first.

- Look for the divine essence in nature. A sunrise, sunset, a mighty tree, the ocean tide, are all ready to reveal their divine essence to you. Next, look for it in the fluttering butterfly, soaring songbird, and the busy squirrel outside your window.

- Look for the divine essence in babies of every kind. Observe the joy, innocence, and trusting nature in babies, children, and even in kittens and puppies and it will be easier to find it in yourself and others.

Forgive quickly, completely, unconditionally

My experience with this has been to simply be willing to forgive and then to ask Love how to do so. These points may help:

- Forgive yourself first. For any, and everything.

- Remember that Love (God) never judges, only humans do. To fully connect to the Love inside you is to abandon, as best you can, the need to judge yourself or others.

- Practice forgiveness in minor situations first: the rude guy at the market, a cross word from a loved one, or a neighbor asking, *again*, to borrow tools that they never return.

Every day, as often as you can, seek guidance from the divine love inside you. Live from there. You can start by asking,

"Love, what would you most have me know today?"

About the Author

Diane L. Haworth, MBA, CHPC is an experienced coach, speaker and author who teaches her clients to consciously connect to the divine within to create a life of "Heart-Centered Success." She is the author of "How to Choose Love When You Just Want to Slap Somebody" as well as the host and creator of the TV show "Heart-Centered Success with Diane L. Haworth" that airs in the Washington, DC area and on YouTube. She lives in the foothills of the beautiful Virginia Blue Ridge Mountains with her husband, Joe, and Rory the cat. She and her husband are close to their grown children and extended family including their beloved grandson, Emory.

To find out more about Diane and her work, visit www.DianeHaworth.com.

A Birth, a Knockout and a Miracle All Within 4 days

Stephan Conradi

My Name is Stephan, and I have lived on the beautiful mediterranean island of Mallorca for about 11 years. I came here because the island seemed to be the perfect match for sports enthusiasts and outdoor lovers. I studied Sport Science at the Sports University in Cologne and after I graduated I decided to go to Central America to learn Spanish. I chose Guatemala because I could afford to take one on one classes.

My trip was open ended and seven months later, when it felt right for me, I realized that it was time to create my own business and life. Central America was wonderful but very far away from Germany and it was difficult to visit my family and friends, so I picked the Spanish island Mallorca, even though I knew very little about it.

I started working on Mallorca in 2008 and my girlfriend Caroline and I opened our outdoor activity business in 2009. We started working 6 months on Mallorca and 6 months in the winter in Germany, which was pretty intense. For me it was a stressful time and I realized, that we were living with one foot in Spain and one foot in Germany, literally. But I took it as something normal, especially during the first 3 years, when I did not expect it to be easy.

In the spring of 2017 I had a very special experience, which turned out to be a wake-up call. I was running an off-road 10km race through mountainous terrain and was about two thirds into it. I hadn't eaten or drunk enough before the race and I was dehydrated. As I made the last climb behind a group of runners I'd been following, I fainted. When I opened my eyes I saw the mountains and a crowd of people around me. At least that's what I think happened because I was in and out of consciousness. A few days later I estimated that I was unconscious for at least 45 minutes, but it might have been longer. The transport from the mountains to the hospital alone could have easily taken 70 minutes.

What I am sure of is that I had a very interesting experience while I was unconscious, although I didn't really understand what was happening. While I lay on the ground, drifting in and out of consciousness, my essence or my spirit, left my body. When I looked down at myself I did not recognize the body below me or realize that it was me. I didn't know what was happening but I was not frightened. Instead I was at ease and relaxed. I thought, "this is the state that needs to be achieved to feel pure bliss and mental calmness."

During the time it took to be transported down from the mountains I had pictures flickering in my mind. My two daughters were three years older and played in front of a house in our village. In another scene I saw a historical building with disco lights and dancing music. I also saw myself at about 2 years old playing in a place where I grew up.

In between all these pictures I saw parts of my body below me, still not recognizing it was me. A little later I felt a pinch on my arm and heard voices, people talking to each other. I could see that the body was in a different position now. Before it was in a seated position and now it was lying down horizontally. I later found out that I was transported down the hill in a car from a neighbour because the roads were too steep for an ambulance. I was then moved to an ambulance that was waiting on a path close the road.

In the ambulance, I heard someone asking me a question in English. "How old are you and where do you come from?" I replied, "I am 97 years old and I am from Bulgaria." I have no idea why I said that.

It was quiet and seemed as though a lot of time was passing. I looked around the ambulance but I couldn't identify anything. Then I felt the body being moved again as I was taken out on the stretcher and into the hospital.

I woke up in the medical consultant room in the hospital in Muro, in the north of Mallorca. Slowly coming to consciousness I looked at my hands and arms and reconnected to my physical self. I saw Caroline enter the room, still beautifully pregnant. We were expecting our second girl at that time. As I became more aware of my surroundings I started to realize what must have happened in the last 90 minutes after I fainted.

The doctors transferred me to the Intensive Care Unit for the first night and kept me for a second night still hooked up to machines to monitor me. I felt fine at that point but I was still confused by this out of body, spiritual experience that had never happened to me before. I was very relaxed, but I was trying to understand what had happened to me. The doctors were also running tests to find out what had happened.

I did not tell the doctors what kind of 'miracle' I experienced, I thought it best to keep this spooky story to myself. I had fainted during the race, because of dehydration and lack of food, but why I told the medical technician that I was 97 years old and from Bulgaria made little sense. Perhaps that was brought on by the dehydration. But that didn't explain my out of body experience.

Around 5:30 a.m the second morning in the hospital, Caroline called to tell me that our baby Juna was coming. The contractions had started and she was going to the hospital in Palma for the birth. We made a plan to meet then go together to the hospital. Caroline's mother Elvira, would drive her and our daughter Lia. I hung up and immediately checked myself out of the hospital and called a taxi.

A few minutes later I met them at the meeting point on the way to the hospital. I hopped into our car, while Elvira and Lia took the taxi home. I drove as patiently as possible to Palma while Caroline's contractions hit the 2-3 minute mark. Right before entering Palma we ended up in traffic. Luckily Juna stayed happily content in Caroline's belly until we arrived at the hospital.

A couple of hours later we had a great natural birth and Juna arrived May 30th, 2017. After the last few days, I was grateful that Caroline and Juna were both healthy and that I was well enough to be with them after my ordeal. But a few days later I slipped into a deep depression, the second one I've had in my life.

During the gloomy summer months I tried to find my way out of my depression. I used techniques that I learned during the first bout of depression such as breathing meditation, mindfulness based stress release, focusing on one thing at a time, yoga and a very structured day. At the beginning of October I was feeling much better and by then it was the end of the season and we closed our shop.

I was relieved to be feeling better emotionally but over the next winter into the beginning of 2018 I was sick quite often. I had a lung disease, a ruptured eardrum, a corneal injury, and started to get neurodermitis, a chronic skin disorder, all within 6 months.

It seemed like these physical symptoms were trying to tell me something, they felt like a wake-up call. Now looking back, I definitely get the message, but I was not quite ready then. It's clear to me now that those physical experiences were signals that were trying to tell me that something had to change, because doing the same things would give me the same results. I had the feeling that I lived in a nutshell the last few years, not being able to use my full potential. These ailments were physical manifestations of my emotional issues and to fully break free of them both I would have to make big changes in my life. I would have to dig deep and find a new path, if I wanted to be happy and emotionally and physically in balance.

Another wake-up call was receiving an email newsletter with an invitation to the European Transformational Teacher's Gathering 2018 in Alicante, Spain. The event was hosted by Steinar Ditlefsen and there would be talks by a couple of great international speakers about physical, spiritual, mental, and emotional transformations. When I arrived at the event, I was surrounded by like-minded people and I felt like I had found something that had been missing in my life. In a way, it felt like coming home. It was such a relief to know that there were people in the world like me, a community of people with a similar mindset, and similar goals, who believe that there is something else besides the physical world.

It was a very intense 3-day seminar for me. The gatherings I had with different seminar participants or speakers made me think a lot. Steinar talked a lot about 'opening your heart' and I have to admit that this seems to be a door opener to plenty of beautiful things in life. Due to the density and quality of the content that was offered in this conference I needed to mentally digest it for a much longer period of time afterward. But when I left the gathering for home I knew that there was a new path for me, one that I had to walk. I felt a new calling, almost a duty, to support, talk, and help other people, who like me, were also going through transformations in their life or simply needed help.

I told Caroline about what happened during the gathering and how I felt a need to make changes in my life. She has always supported me and we agreed to go on this journey together. The summer season was almost upon us and we already had a couple of commitments, so we decided to keep our company going for the 10th season.

Since the beginning of the 2018 season we have put the business up for sale and committed to our new path. I know that I am on the right path and I will continue to walk it. It feels so right although what I am doing is nothing special. I am literally just expressing what I think and feel and sharing my experiences.

It is so great to see and feel what matters. I could hang out the whole day just observing my two little daughters. The way they see and explore the world is full of magic. This is what matters to me, to see the beauty and magic in everything that is around you. I see and feel that everything is somehow connected to each other. A complete new view and perspective opened up within me. I am very sure that this would not have happened if I had finished the running competition like the years before, tired but happy that I made it to the finish line.

With writing this story, posting videos and blog articles, I want to make people realize that changing our mind can change our life. After my out of body experience I know that the physical and spiritual planes are closely connected. For me it was a miraculous experience which I had never in my life experienced. It had an incredible impact on me. Since then, I am looking at myself and life in general from a different angle.

Making a change starts with the decision to do so. To that end I am trying to create a new life in the future whilst dealing with the present and being happy with everything that has happened, the good and the bad. I am grateful for all the experiences that I've had especially the painful ones. I would like to create a bridge between the physical and the spiritual worlds to draw attention to this connection. I am supported by my family and amazing mentors who are helping me do this.

I have twice gone through bouts of deep depression. During those times I was almost numb and didn't feel anything, so now pain is as welcome as joy; one doesn't truly exist without the other. My path now is to create physical and digital content about change processes, that can be easily shared. My plan is to publish articles, ebooks, videos, video courses, podcasts and interviews. I also want to speak on stage to connect with people and create another way of thinking that helps us to see the world in a new way.

I want to give hope, that in every darkness lies a light, even you don't yet see it. I want to create workshops to not only connect with people, but also to connect people with themselves again. Combining this with experiences in nature will be a powerful connection. In my life journey I have learned that 3 elements help to create a balance within us: The breath, the mind, and the physical. Yoga combines all of these. Practicing the 3 elements separately at first, might help people to start, then later on they can combine them through yoga practises.

We all have our own history, perception, and problems, but it's up to us to decide if we want to suffer or if we want to be happy, blissful, and open. We have to start by understanding that we can create that future. We only have to decide to make a change. I want to help create that change and to shape that future.

About the Author

The out of body experience opened my eyes and my heart to an invisible world which surrounds us all. There is a lot of scientific proof that our mind and our thoughts can change physical reality. I have no doubt of this fact. If we can dream and turn this dream into reality later, isn't that also an act of magic somehow?

I described in *"Life after Trauma"*, a book compiled by Dr. Andrea Pennington, how I experienced a change just by looking into someone's eyes. So please get out there, with an open mind and an open heart and let the magic happen.

If you are interested in my work, please check out my website or social media channels:
www.stephanconradi.com
www.facebook.com/pleaseshine
www.instagram.com/stephanconradi

The Suitcase

Gitte Winter Graugaard

My father was and still today is a brilliant storyteller. I remember those childhood evenings with him reading to me so clearly. I would crawl into my bed and he would sit next to me and introduce me to a world of fairy tales. He would become different characters and make the story fly from the pages and into my bedroom. He brought to life the wonderful tales created by the brilliant authors who knew how to create magic in books for children to hold in their hearts. I would swim with the ugly duckling to the big pond, go deep into the woods with Ronia, the Robber's Daughter, and cry with Cinderella when her evil stepsisters left her behind. How could they be so cruel?

My father's joy in reading to me made me a part of the stories too and the characters became my friends. Teaching me as a child to fall in love with books provided me with endless adventures filled with magic and wonder.

My mother would take me and my sister to the local library and I loved it. I still remember the smell of that library. When we went on vacation we would drive from Denmark to Southern France. I carried boxes of tapes with audio books from the library to listen to on my Walkman or even better on the car radio together with the rest of my family. As we drove for days through Germany into Switzerland and France, hour after hour, Ivanhoe, Anne of Green Gables, Laura from The Little House on the Prairie or Robin Hood accompanied me and made the long boring car ride so much more adventurous.

Thanks to my father and my love of books, my sense of creativity was strong when I was a child, and I especially loved writing. I was a natural storyteller. My diaries were long and detailed and I even enjoyed writing essays for school in multiple languages. I played the piano, played theater, sang in a children's choir, played with dolls, recorded stories on my cassette player, and baked cakes to sell on the street to the neighbourhood kids.

The garden of my childhood home was enchanting, with lots of nooks and hiding places, beautiful flowers, juicy berries and ripe fruit on wild bushes and old trees. My mother was always to be found weeding somewhere in our huge and seemingly never-ending garden. In the summertime we literally lived in the garden, and used to hoist the meals outside in a large basket on a rope from the kitchen window on the first floor down into the garden. Joyfully my sister, friends and I jumped from our swings into, what seemed to be, the largest sandpit in the world. We built secret caves in the back of the garden, slept in tents, biked to the beach to swim, made bonfires and grilled twisted bread on sticks. In many ways the characters from the books I read or movies I watched were with me while playing. The characters had become my imaginary friends and made me play for hours on my own.

Sometimes my imagination would also lead me into trouble or fear. As I played with different imaginary characters "we" would for instance steal cookies from the kitchen and get into trouble. Trying to make my imaginary friends take the blame didn't help much, when my mother lifted her eyebrow!

I also vividly remember the troll phase of my childhood, when I was certain that my parents were actually trolls and my older sister was about to grow into trollhood - the stage of becoming an adult troll. The troll scenes would play out at night when Rikke, my sister, was allowed to stay up longer than me.

That was so unfair that I thought they must have been up to something very important which I was certain they were hiding from me. My imagination led me to believe that my parents and my sister in her teens were part of a secret troll society you could only join at a certain age. I would try to sneak up on my troll family after they had sent me to bed (several times), but every time they somehow managed to hear me and turned into their normal human self again. Despite many attempts I never managed to reveal their true troll identity. "Go back to bed, Gitte", my mother would say.

At the age of 12 my excitement for reading led me to take a job at the school library. I would walk the aisles dragging my finger from one book to the next — leaving a bit of a dust print behind — imagining I could keep all the wisdom of my favourite writers in my chest. I loved the smell of a new book — I still do. Those days in the school library created a dream in me that one day I too could become a writer and share beautiful tales with children to hold in their hearts. I felt lucky to know about other dimensions at that young age. And I couldn't imagine a world without access to these other spheres.

However, as the years went by and I got into high school and later business school, studying slowly took all my time. I was less focused on being creative and more on getting good grades and making it in the corporate world. Looking back at those many years of studying it was all about trying to remember what some wise person had once said about something clever, instead of figuring out what I thought myself. I wonder how many students can say that their university years were full of creativity and not only about repeating somebody else's thoughts or theories. I wish students were taught more about the art of reflection and how to access inspiration rather than the importance of repetition.

My first and only year working in an advertising company wasn't magical either. I had recently gotten married to the love the my life in a big wedding with friends and family, and we decided that the time had come for us to have a baby. Having lived in many different countries before, we thought, "why not take my maternity leave abroad on some exotic destination, where my husband could find work?" When he and I manifest together and from our hearts our dreams often come true. Shortly after we moved to Croatia to grow our family with our daughter in my womb.

As the waves of the Adriatic Sea rolled to the shore and thousands of stars lit up the dark night sky I caressed my belly loving my unborn child. Right there I realised that now was the first time since my long childhood summers that I had the opportunity to create and endless time to do it. It was one of those crossroads.

In those months the waves and the sun inspired me to listen to my heart. When I did, I heard an old familiar voice whispering to me reminding me of my childhood and encouraged me to write some of my beloved memories down. I realized that my parents had given me both deep roots to connect to something deep inside of me, strong wings to fly out to seek adventures, and a clear intuition to always follow my heart. The voices also reminded me about my old dream of becoming a writer. Maybe now was the time

When we moved to Croatia I also started studying personal development. I read Louise Hay, Wayne Dyer, and Esther Hicks. They too became my friends. They still are, even though some of them have gone to heaven to continue their work from above. I began my own meditation practice. In my meditations I connected to the baby girl in my womb. It felt like the child growing inside of me somehow connected me to my own inner child. And through her I also reconnected to my vivid imagination and creativity.

One particular day on the beach, I went into a deep meditation. I always fly to other hemispheres in my meditations and this day was no exception. I remember bright purple light, white clouds, waterfalls and the feeling of connecting to something wiser outside of me.

During a ceremony in that meditation I received an old brown suitcase. Later that day I closed my eyes and imagined placing the suitcase on a table in front of me. Slowly with my heart pounding I opened it. An amazing world appeared to me from inside the suitcase. It was full of dreams, hopes and fairytales. It felt like my entire imagination from my childhood, with all those amazing tales my father had told me, had been waiting in that suitcase for me to find it and to spark my imagination again. Now I was the adult. A child was growing inside of me. I had all the time in world to begin telling tales of my own.

The suitcase, gave me access to an imaginary world, complete with landscapes, colours, characters and emotions. Stories would come alive as I watched the characters interact and live their lives right there in the suitcase — like watching a theater or a movie. I would then write down their story sometimes asking my new friends to stop talking so fast, as my fingers furiously tap danced across the keyboard in a desperate bid to keep up. The suitcase gave me access to my creativity. All I had to do was close my eyes and let my imagination flow.

For the next years I kept my magical suitcase close by. We moved our little family from the sunny beach in Croatia to a winter wonderland in Canada, where our second daughter was born. My life was busy being a full-time mother to my two precious young girls. But as soon as they were asleep I would close my eyes, open the suitcase, and start typing. In the beginning I remember holding my heart in my hands as I opened the suitcase hoping so intensely that the characters hadn't vanished. Hoping that I hadn't lost access to them, to my imagination. But every time, no matter how long time had passed, they were waiting for me. And I am forever grateful for this.

The suitcase was also how I opened up to channeling stories that I came to share as an author later on. At that stage I still didn't know much about channeling and I couldn't separate my feeling of being creative from the feeling of being inspired. Or 'In spiritus' as my dear friend, Dr. Andrea Pennington would say.

The story I wrote to my daughters turned into my first children's book "Pink Cloud and Murky Bastards" — a pre-puberty crime novel. The suitcase was my magical token, my portkey — my Narnia wardrobe — my magical portal to not only my own imagination and creativity but also to channeling from something larger than me — from source.

Today, many books later, my skill of channeling has become much stronger and many of the books I write today are made much more from channeling than as products of my imagination. I often sit back with the question: "Who wrote this?" when I read my own books. I am here to help children thrive and I am told what to write in order to help parents help their children through my books.

My magical suitcase came to me through meditation — and it is no coincidence that I channel most of my books into children's meditations today. As a kid I dreamed of one day being able to help children open up to more dimensions and spheres. Today I understand that the worlds and spheres I open up for children are not outside of them, but inside as inner landscapes for them to access and understand through meditation, in what I call The Valley of Hearts. As children today grow up having easy access to everything around them, they can fly to multiple countries, live in globalised cities, eat eggs and bacon for breakfast, sushi for lunch, and curry dishes for dinner, play computer games and watch too much tv — they don't need more entertainment. What they desperately need is to understand their inner beauty, the strength and resources they have inside and the dimensions and magic of their inner landscapes.

To this day the suitcase is very dear to me but I no longer need it as a portal. My creative source now lives within me and has become a large part of me and my everyday life. My interest in personal development also led me to become a life mastery coach, a healer and I have served as a Lightworker the past five years. I assist my clients into a meditation and I guide them through their inner landscape and open up to their spirituality by working with vibrations, healing, heart energy and channeling.

Many of my clients also receive magical tokens like my suitcase in their sessions. Most often they are handed a tool, such as a key or a book or something from nature, given to them by an avatar or a human. They can also meet a wise animal with a message, or get reacquainted with a loved one in heaven who shares something with them. It feels like the tokens they are given hold a message for them to know how to take the next step forward and to grow emotionally or spiritually to share their love and light with the world. The tokens help them lift their vibrations and transform their lives. The tokens are full of supporting energy from source, so beautiful, so powerful, so magical.

I am curious to better understand how we can consciously access these tokens even better and also teach children to find them deep inside like the most important treasure hunt they will ever embark on. I believe we receive the tokens we are ready for if we consciously look for them. Being conscious is the key in a world where many people seem to be sleeping and steering their lives from a stage of unconscious autopiloting.

For me the magic in my life started early in my childhood as my father helped my imagination come alive. In fact much of my childhood seems magical to me today. The act of being born is magical in itself. We are all miracles — even if many of us sadly have forgotten it. So close your eyes for a moment and cherish the fact that you too are a miracle to this world.

Every day I strive to hold onto the child inside of me and stay childlike. When my daughter said to me, "You're still a child, mum. You still play and have fun every day in your work!" To me, it was the best compliment ever.

Much of the magic of life happens when we stop being so adult-like, practical, responsible, well behaved, and to be frank, boring. So much of the sparkle in life happens around children, animals and childlike adults. The more creativity I let into my life — through singing, playing the piano, drawing with my girls, creating delicious and beautiful meals, painting, growing vegetables and flowers my garden, speaking on stages, working as a Lightworker — the more creative channels I open up.

Meditation is the best way for me to access my heart, my creative source and my magic. I let go and drift into my inner world that connects me through spirit with places I have never been. And when I go there, I remember that being human on this amazing planet is magical in itself. It inspires me to share my magic with the world and encourage other people to share theirs as well. Because when we share from our hearts we light up the world and each other. And that is really all the magic we need.

Please, share your light with the world. We can't wait to see you, hear you, feel your energy, and enjoy the beauty you bring to the world.

About the Author

Gitte Winter Graugaard, is a bestselling author, life coach, energy mentor, and Lightworker (*Roomforreflection.com*) from Denmark. She is on a mission to aid parents in helping their children to thrive through child meditation and mindfulness. Gitte is also the founder of the Momo Academy (*www.momo-academy.com*), which enables schools to offer mindfulness, meditation and yoga to their pupils as part of their education through a beautiful growing network of Lightworkers.

Gitte also coaches adults to believe in their magic, share their light, become more creative, and sparkle more in life. She is an international speaker and facilitates workshops all over her home country and abroad.

Check out Gitte's blog at www.RoomforReflection.com and at www.facebook.com/roomforreflectionint

From Rock Bottom to Abundance, Love, and Light

Margaretha Tosi-Lesman

It was a lovely spring day in April 2004, the sun was shining through the glass, spreading light and warmth into the living room. I opened the garden door and breathed in the lovely spring air. Energized, I turned on some music and started my morning chores. While vacuuming I started to feel frustrated and angry. I knew those feelings very well but always kept them inside, afraid of what might happen if I let them out. At that moment the vacuum cleaner stopped working. It didn't move how I wanted it to move and I snapped. In that instance all the built up frustration, anger, hurt and disappointment, mostly towards myself, came to the surface and I blacked out.

Coming to my senses a few minutes later, I looked at the vacuum cleaner cord in amazement. In my rage I had yanked the cord so hard that I had taken off a part of the wall with it. That's when it hit me that my rage and frustration, were completely out of proportion.

I needed to take action. But how, where, who could I turn to? Feeling ashamed about my emotions, especially my rage, I closed myself up again. I shut down and hid behind the wall I created to keep functioning. I knew exactly what I was doing and what I was thinking. I just didn't have the courage nor the tools to deal with it or talk about it. Feeling ashamed kept me in that space for over half a year. And when I look back, I can see that it was much longer than that. There had been other smaller occurrences that had built up towards this huge blackout, but again, all inside of myself.

That afternoon my mum came to visit and saw the hole in the wall. I was so worried that she would be angry with me that I broke down. I cried so hard I could barely speak. I was finally able to explain to her how confused I felt but I couldn't find the right words to explain what was going on. The only thing I knew was that I couldn't continue living like this. I was so grateful when my mum held me, softly shushed me and told me it was okay. "I've seen this coming," she said. "You've been struggling for quite some time and I didn't know how to reach out to help you."

I felt so relieved. There was no rejection, no anger only understanding. After we had a cup of tea together she handed me a small piece of paper she had found hanging on a bulletin board at a local shop, that had a phone number written on it and two words: "Surrendering and Struggling". Even though I wanted to deny they resonated with me I knew it was the truth. I had been struggling for so long, it was time to surrender.

Those words and that little piece of paper led me to a lovely psycho-energetic coach who helped me through some deep rooted limiting beliefs and behaviour that I have been able to acknowledge and let go of. Always feeling not enough, or less if you will, than others, less smart or successful than others. And a quitter for not finishing an education in order to become a psychiatric nurse, 5 months before graduation. At that moment I just couldn't — a patient's suicide triggered memories of a former boyfriend's suicide attempt, it was all just too much to handle at the age of 20.

Within half a year of our first meeting I decided that I wanted to support others in the same way so I started a holistic coaching education that has since changed my life. It has brought me closer to myself, to knowing myself on a level that I had never known before. I learned to trust my inner instincts and accept all my spirituality with love.

Yet I was still not able to break the cycle I'd been in for many years because limiting beliefs kept me where I was. I was unhappy in a 7 year relationship that took me 2 more years to break out of. I wasn't getting what I needed in the relationship, there was no intimacy, or physical affection, and I felt like I was dying inside, yet felt powerless to leave. People who know me know that I love cuddles and hugs. And living with someone who froze every time I tried to give or receive them, hurt me to my core and I felt rejected every time I tried. So I stopped trying and something inside me died.

The aftermath was not pretty, having to sell the house we owned together, not agreeing on so many things made me want to escape from the whole situation and that's exactly what I did. I escaped into the arms of a man who seemed to have everything I had been missing for the last 9 years. He was warm, cuddly, loved hugs and was always there for me, or so I thought, even though I had a deep instinctive feeling of doubt and mistrust towards him. I had been cheated on before but I decided to ignore my inner wisdom and just go with it. I really wanted this escape to work.

We were going on wonderful trips, had lovely dinners, and I was getting spoiled with clothes, jewelry, handbags. A girl's dream come true. I still had those feelings of mistrust tugging and pulling on me but again I ignored my inner wisdom.

But those feeling persisted and I couldn't shake them. So I started checking his phone and found the most disgusting texts to and from other women that he had obviously been with. When I confronted him he said I was overreacting and I was wrong for going through his phone and for not trusting him. I got it all wrong he said. It was not after he stepped it up a notch and became really disrespectful towards me that I had enough. I left him because I just couldn't anymore.

I was heartbroken and happy at the same time. I took a few belongings and moved out of our apartment.

I decided to take a break from relationships with men and work on the relationship I had with myself. Specifically, the one of being alone with me, myself and I. I bought an apartment and made it mine. There are many times I just wanted to pick up the phone to my ex and invite him back because I was so lonely. Fortunately, I have a dear bestie Xaviera, and we've always agreed that if you have the urge to call someone "who did you wrong, call me first." And so I did… many times. Each time she helped me on my way to healing. Being able to be alone and happy is a gift only I could give myself.

In 2012 I was starting to enjoy life again and after being single for 2 years, I was ready for the right man in my life and I knew the universe was listening. After being on my own my connection with the universe or the divine had gotten stronger. One evening I sat on my sofa in my small but cosy apartment and made a list of 'desires' for the love of my life. He needs to be honest, loyal, trustworthy, a family man and a man. Not being specific about where he would live, I then sent my lovely list to the universe with love and blowing out a candle that had accompanied me throughout the ritual of writing the list of desires.

Simultaneously I had been researching my Italian roots from my father's side. After the search for who I really was, it became so important to discover my roots and the truth behind the family secret that my father was born out of a love relationship during the second world war. The secret that he was not the child of my Dutch grandfather had been hanging over our family for more than 60 years.

Looking back now, it was one of the few moments in life where I chose to listen to my instincts and my heart consciously and to move forward even though not everyone was happy about me going on this search. I respectfully asked my father if he would be okay with it and I got his approval. Though it was after I had already booked the tickets to Italy.

While booking all the tickets and hotels for my travel to Italy, I happened to come across a lovely Italian man through the internet. He ticked all the boxes, plus he was good looking. He happened to be coming to The Netherlands, where I lived, the week before I was to travel to Italy so we decided to meet at the airport.

When he came out of the gate I knew immediately that he was The One. As I watched him walk toward me, I saw images of us getting married, having children, and creating a wonderful life together. But I wasn't going to tell him that on our first date! He would have jumped right back on that plane (or at least that's what I thought).

He helped me unravel our family secret in 4 days and we fell madly in love. Four amazing days is all it took to feel that calm and peace in my heart, soul and being. We were let into all old military archives in Modena, the municipality gave more information than they were actually allowed to give and I understood there and then that we were helped in spirit by my biological paternal grandfather.

Right before I travelled back to The Netherlands I told him that I loved him and was anxious for his reply. Tears pooled in his eyes and he told me he loved me too. My heart jumped for joy. The man that I had been asking for, had arrived.

I needed to be patient as we travelled one year back and forth between Milan and Groningen. Seeing each other every other week our longing for each other grew out of proportion. He asked me to marry him half a year into our relationship and we married a year later in The Netherlands with all our beloved family and friends nearby. I wanted to have my dear grandmother present when we sealed our love, a love that perhaps would not have existed if she would not have fallen in love with her Italian man. I praise my grandmother every day for giving life to my father in brutal circumstances and for deciding to keep my father when my grandmother's family demanded her to give my father up for adoption. And I praise her every day for her bravery and motherly instincts right after WWII as a single mum of 21 years young.

After our wedding I moved to Italy. Leaving everything I'd ever known behind, I quit a well-paid management job, emptied my apartment and went — just like that — knowing in my heart it was the right step with the right man. Learning to trust my instincts in smaller instances helped me to trust it in on bigger life changing ones like this. A month later we took a nice trip to visit Rome and 3 weeks later we discovered I was pregnant. The baby was so welcomed that I knew she would close my family's circle of shame and secrecy.

After my daughter was born motherhood hit me hard sometimes, more specifically the loneliness that came with it. My husband had to go back to work a week after the birth and there I was with a little one in a country that still didn't feel was mine yet and my Italian was not very good.

I managed to find friends and build up a social network along with building up my own business in Milan with HypnoBirthing. I was one of the first in the country to teach this wonderful philosophy to expecting parents in order to be able to birth their babies in an empowered, calm and gentle way. A way in which I strongly believe we can change the world.

One year into motherhood I decided to become a Doula. I would support expecting parents and new parents during the last phase of the pregnancy, labor, birth, and afterwards. Something that I had really needed during my postpartum period.

Four years into motherhood with a new level of womanhood I have been able to expand my life in Italy, I have created dear friendships and an even closer connection to my husband and daughter. Knowing that my family is my base and foundation helps me create an even deeper level of intuition, strength, and self-confidence.

Having helped so many women and couples find their way into parenting made me want to expand my wings even further. I didn't know how until I was part of an amazing spiritual teachers training in Spain where I had the most wondrous vision I've ever had. I still remember the moment of connecting to our amazing mother earth and love, shaking and crying because I know it was true... We are LOVE. Having had the courage to share my vision during the training and talking about it has expanded my being in an amazing way and I'm determined to carry out my vision in order to help make the world a better place.

I have seen the possibilities open up when a woman allows herself to be held through and with this level of love. During these embraces, that I've called 'Simply Embraced', women are invited to let go of all of their pain, they are given the space to be themselves, to let go of shame, guilt, and striving for perfection.

This is how we can stop generations of struggling and suffering from our family karma, baggage, and shame. This is how we as women can step into and own our amazing womanhood. This is how we can come closer together instead of further apart. I see how the future can look when my bold vision comes true.

Imagine what this could do for our health throughout our lives, our hormone balance, and our possibility to conceive without medical intervention. Tapping into our own wisdom instead of tapping into the need for outside resources.

Imagine what this could do for young women growing up in our world today, feeling supported by other strong and self-loving women, empowering them to be as beautiful and strong as they are. Imagine teaching them by actions instead of subconscious programming through commercials on TV because our actions will speak louder than those words. I can imagine a world where women lift each other up to new levels of empowerment and self-love.

We as women are so strong and I believe we are strongest when we combine our strengths with love. This is when we can change the world.

This is what I'm committed to do with my time and my life and all the experiences I've had so far. I am creating this space for women wherever I go, holding a safe and enclosed space to release in, releasing what is blocking from stepping into their power, stepping into who we really are... beautiful loving and strong human beings.

Much love,

Margaretha Tosi – Lesman

About the Author

Margaretha Tosi-Lesman is a thought leader, a HypnoBirthing Practitioner, a Doula, and a Spiritual Coach. She supports women and couples through pregnancy, birth and afterwards. She lives near Milan, Italy and works in the whole north area to support foreigners in this important phase of their lives. Being the bridge between 2 cultures and 2 or more languages she's always able to create balance during a somewhat hectic period in couples' lives.

She's a safe haven and very much in contact with our Mother Earth. With her Simply Embraced technique she's able to create a safe space wherein you are allowed to release and let go of all hurt and pain that you are able and willing to let go of in order to step into your full power of self.

For HypnoBirthing visit www.hypnobirthingitalia.com or www.facebook.com/hypnobirthingwithmargaretha

For Simply Embraced visit www.margarethatosi.com

Or contact her via email margarethatosi@gmail.com

Delusions of the Mind
Ascension Into Spirit

Kimberly L. Wright

An Excerpt

I'm about to share a story that I believed to be my life story until I went to Peru and began my awakening through drinking sacred plant medicine Ayahuasca. This ancient medicinal plant is blended into a shamanic tea and used by shamans for healing people with addictions and emotional traumas. It also enables the expansion of consciousness that creates a connection to our soul, our guides and to God.

Before I share my story, I have a few questions for you. What if, after living your life into adulthood, God told you that everything you thought you experienced wasn't true and everything experienced was seen through a programmed lens, a download, a lens that's created from our family, from others, and we are unaware we are looking through?

What if you meet God at first as an external experience but then as an internal one where the appearance of life is fully explained, what would you do? How would your life be different if you were told everything you thought you experienced in the way you experienced it wasn't true? Would know who you were without that history? Would you know how to mourn and release your experience? If you found out you are God what would it change and would you allow it?

Within these pages is part of my story, and until February 2018 the majority of what I'm writing I believed was true. I mean how could it not be? I experienced it, didn't I? I welcome you to join me on this journey into our truth, but first it may help you to experience how the delusion was created and how far down the rabbit hole a person can go.

A Troubled Beginning

I don't know if my mother had intended to get pregnant again, because when I was 15 my mother told me that had abortions been legal she would've had one. It wasn't until my mother passed away six years ago that my cousin told me my mother's confession, which really created an understanding for me as to why the things that happened when I was born happened.

My mother said, "I'm not sure if this is why Kimberly and I never got along but when I was in the hospital giving birth to her, Connor," my father, "brought in his mistress to live in my home." When she came home with me after being in the hospital several weeks my brother said, "Mommy, daddy had this woman staying here." She told my cousin, "in that moment I wanted nothing to do with Kimberly."

I can only assume that she thought if she hadn't been pregnant maybe he wouldn't have cheated on her. Perhaps she believed that I was the cause of him cheating on her.

I have to wonder telling this next part of the story, now knowing her confession, if my mother wanting nothing to do with me was the real reason they would lock me in my room for years. I know that when she was intoxicated later in my life, she would say how horrible it was for her to hear me crying, begging to be let out of the room when no one come. She said that sometimes it was hard to push the door back because as I got older I would lay down at the crack of the door begging them to let me out, or for someone to come in. I would fall asleep there and they would have to push the door back. She said that the reason they made that decision was because I didn't sleep very much and they wanted me to sleep.

When I was around five or six I discovered that I could lift the window and climb out of it. I went and knocked on the front door, and from that moment on I wasn't locked in my room again. I can only imagine what went through my mind being abandoned like that, being unloved, because no matter how you look at it, that is what happened.

I didn't speak until I was three, I grunted, they all thought there was something wrong with me because I didn't talk, they believed that maybe that happened because the umbilical cord was wrapped around my neck when I was born and maybe I had brain damage.

When I did start to talk I just walked around saying I wanted to die. In second grade my teacher asked for someone to evaluate my home situation, the school sent a psychologist into my parents' house to do an evaluation because no child that's 7 years old should walk around saying she wanted to die. My mother stated that she had been getting a lot of flak from other members of the family because of how I behaved, I wouldn't sit still, I was into everything and they found that very irritating and felt that she needed to control me better. She wanted a dainty, docile daughter, and that is not how I behaved.

They were been beating me a lot, hoping to control my behavior, and I said, "You can't make me cry". I was born without tears. I've always believed that God did that for me, because if they had known I was crying when they were beating me, they would've beat me longer. I do know that I made the decision that I wasn't going to cry, I was not going to give them the satisfaction of knowing they were hurting me.

The end of the report said, "Something needs to be done to help this child or something bad is going to happen". Nobody could do anything, I came from an upper-middle-class home, they had jobs, there was no outward appearance of abuse.

No matter where I went I was tortured. The neighborhood kids refused to play with me. In order to be able to play with them I had to go up to Mrs. Simpson's house, ring the doorbell and pull my pants down. They thought it was funny and afterward, they'd beat me up anyway. But I kept going back, begging them to spend time with me. I didn't understand what they thought was wrong with me, why wouldn't they just be my friends. It seemed no matter where I went no one wanted to have anything to do with me.

Drugs and Loneliness

It was just a matter of time before I turned to drugs and at age 13 I did just that. Drugs provided the only way I knew to escape my feelings; they also gave me a connection to other people. When I had drugs, people wanted to spend time with me. I didn't realize until much later that the only reason they were spending time with me was because I had drugs.

I desperately wanted to not feel alone, so I did anything I had to do, from performing oral sex or hand jobs, to forging my parents' checks for cash, or stealing my parents' silver and pawning it, just to get drugs so I could maintain a connection to people and to not feel.

For me, it wasn't even about the drugs. Well, some of it was because I didn't want to feel my feelings, but more than that it was really about not feeling alone. That's an interesting thing for those of us who do drugs: we never get exactly what it is we are looking for – an escape. I remained a virgin during this time because I refused to be with someone who didn't love me. I knew even back then that if someone said "I love you" while doing drugs, it wasn't true. Love spoken while doing alcohol and drugs is not love. I always had a knowing around this even on drugs.

I didn't know how to extract myself from the cycle of drugs. I was lonely and confused and often very angry because of all the unconsciousness of other people. When I was 15, my mother overheard me talking to my boyfriend on the phone and believed I was going to kill them, so she had me committed to a state mental institution. Thus, began my life in foster homes, juvenile detention, numerous drug charges, felony conviction and 32 drug programs by the time I was 21.

The final moment came when I was 22 and I just couldn't live with myself any longer. I didn't know how to stop creating my own pain so I decided to kill myself. I broke into an ex-boyfriend's house and stole his gun. I decided to call a crisis center because I wanted someone to feel what it was like to be me. I didn't realize that the woman at the center had called the police after tracing my telephone call. The SWAT team had surrounded the house with a report of a suicidal woman with a gun. The odd thing is that I had a knowing that told me to hide the gun under the sofa and within seconds the glass started to break and there were police standing around me in the den of my parents' home.

I wasn't being arrested, just detained until a temporary detention order could be obtained based on me trying to kill myself. They called the judge in the middle the night and he told them to put me in a holding cell and he would deal with me during the following morning court recess.

It was the longest four hours believing that at any moment I was going to prison because I was a felon with a gun that I had stolen. When I walked into the judge's office, I told him that I was sorry and that I knew he was going to put me in prison. He said, "young lady I don't know if there was a gun, we didn't find it. You're already in your own prison and if you want to kill yourself I'm not going to stop you." He walked out of his office and left me sitting there by myself.

In that moment, I realized for the first time that there was no one left to call, I had burned all my bridges. When I went back to my parents' house I realized I had a decision to make, I decided that I would try to get clean for six months and if nothing changed I would kill myself.

The Beginning of Freedom

At age 22, I went to AA, Alcoholics Anonymous. A woman named Georgette told me that she wanted to be my sponsor, but I had to move in with her and her husband, because she said there was no way I would ever get my shit together living with my parents. While living there I decided I needed something to do. My inner knowing told me to make business cards that read

"Wright Cleaning" with my phone number. On the back of each card, I wrote "$45". I then placed a card on every resident's door in the condominium complex.

Several weeks later, the management company called to tell me I was not allowed to solicit, but they had properties all over Virginia and offered for me to work for them. The only hitch was I needed a $10 million insurance policy, which I certainly could not afford. One day on my way to the beach, I saw a sign for an insurance company outside a small house. I went inside and told the agent/owner my life story and that I needed an insurance policy and asked the cost. He offered to write me a fake policy to help me start my business. He told me that if anything happened, if they filed a claim, he would say that I'd stopped making my payments. It was total synchronicity!

It was an ending but also a beginning. I had learned to live without drugs but my emotional wounds created an undercurrent that would affect my life for another 30 years. I believed only someone outside of myself could make me feel complete. For many years, in various relationships, I dated a version of my mother. The women were extremely critical, wounded, and would lash out at me emotionally. As I developed more self-esteem I still gravitated to disconnected women, but they were more loving and accepting of me. I dated people according to how I felt about myself, they were only mirrors.

In April 2017, my last relationship ended, I bought my first home, and I stopped seeking relationships outside of myself to define who I was. I had finally hit bottom. Then my inner knowing said it was time to write my story, and that by the time my story came out, I would be ready for what would come.

I was not prepared for what came next.

Journeys Into Awakening

I was led to Kyra Baehr, a preacher who exuded everything I wanted to be. Her open, loving spirit called to me, so I messengered her on Facebook after learning she had a spiritual coaching business called LiveLightToday.com. What happened the next 3 months was nothing short of life changing. I had never had counseling like this, she took me on soul retrieval journeys, rebirthing journeys, and breath work sessions which created the beginning of an awakening that I didn't know existed. This opened the gateway to what would come next: ayahuasca, sacred plant medicine, which revealed through visions, a gateway to God and to my Truth.

I had been planning a vacation to Peru and my inner knowing told me to, Google 'spiritual experiences Peru.' What came up were listings of ayahuasca retreats. I read that drinking ayahuasca takes you on a 'journey', which "removes blocks to your truth" by allowing you to see them and process them. This scared me because I believed I had suppressed childhood memories and I was afraid of what I might learn. But there was never a part of me that wasn't willing to drink medicine. I knew that if I was going to help people I had to be willing to go to any lengths myself.

In February 2018, I went alone for six days to an ayahuasca retreat in Peru and during my medicine journeys I met God. I was shown that there is nothing that is not of God. Two weeks after returning from Peru I went to another retreat in Costa Rica to drink plant medicine again. That is where I found the truth about who and what I am and who and what we are.

The truth of who and what we are is this: We are God experiencing itself through this form and these experiences. Regardless of what my human self experienced, there is a soul within that wasn't touched by those experiences, was never hurt or betrayed, and was always loved.

During my ayahuasca journey God said this to me… "The inner child is not what we have been programmed to believe it is. It's actually our soul, and has the DNA blueprint of the entire universe imprinted on it. It comes here to experience life, and everything that it experiences has a shock absorber around it. It doesn't get infected or affected by anything that it experiences; it's just experiencing."

Be in the world but not of the world!

That's the way it was in the beginning of our soul's experience in this dimension. After we are born, then the 'downloads' begin, creating personhood and the belief in who we are. The downloads come from others, the beliefs that if you had a traumatic childhood, your partner left you, or you were unloved…etc., you were a wounded person. In truth, the downloads aren't real and they create a whole separate personality that is not attached whatsoever to the original DNA of who and what we are. That personality is actually what we *believe* we are, it creates the *belief* that we are a person having an experience. When in actuality we're God experiencing itself.

The whole personality structure consists of downloads/beliefs given to us by others who also believe that what they experience is real. None of this is real. God's name isn't even God. God doesn't have a name. Nothing does. Innocence, love, spontaneity, joy, the inquisitive nature, the pure ability to see beyond anything that happens to the beauty within it, just to name a few — all of *that* is what we are. Everything else is just a download.

Allow the mourning of what was believed to be experienced to occur with love and grace, open yourself to your true expression, love. And know you are always loved.

What if you were shown you are God? What in your life would change and would you allow it?

About the Author

Kimberly L. Wright knew all along that her life would be anything but mundane and meaningless. A troubled childhood and rebellious adolescence led her into adulthood as a successful entrepreneur with a collection of dysfunctional relationships.

This gave her life a compelling story, but Kimberly realized she was always more than that. Being led to drink plant medicine, she met and talked with God which led her to a personal awakening.

Kimberly L Wright is spiritual guide who facilitates private and group sessions that give participants an opportunity to open the awareness of what exists beyond the physical world, to their truth is within.

Coming soon the full version of her story in the book "Delusions of the Mind Ascension Into Spirit"

Connect with Kimberly online and via email:
kimberly@kimberlylwright.com
www.KimberlyLWright.com

The Mystical Experience That Set Me Free From Depression*

Andrea Pennington, MD, C.Ac

I n August of 2005 I asked God to take my life.

After an impromptu vocal performance in a dreamy night club in St. Tropez, France, exhilarated but confused, I was ready for my life to be over. No, I wasn't drunk or drugged. I was so blissed out from temporarily living the life I *really* wanted, that I didn't want to go on living the miserable life I had before.

The irony is, from the outside, it appeared that I had an ideal life. Back in the United States I had a beautiful home, a sexy convertible car, a million-dollar business and plenty of money in the bank. Only three years into my professional career I'd already published my first book, appeared on *Oprah — multiple times* — and I was slightly famous.

As "America's Empowerment Doctor" I was known for setting people free from disease, depression and dead-end careers. I had people coming to see me from far and wide to help them heal and have a fabulous life, like mine. I regularly appeared in magazines and TV talk shows flashing a bright smile from ear to ear.

But my smile did not reflect true happiness. Not at all. On the inside I was miserable. Nobody could tell, of course. When my career seemed to be at an all-time high and I had everything that one would consider worthwhile, I was utterly miserable. It was painful because I didn't like who I had become. My media image was that of a prudish know-it-all who wasn't following her own advice: "Honor your dreams, for they are the treasures of your soul."

Yeah, right! In truth I'm a performing artist with a medical degree — an actress who *played* a doctor on TV. Yet, I wasn't honoring *my* dream to sing, act, and perform. Instead I secretly lived with depression for over a decade.

Every day I struggled to put on that happy smile before leaving the house to face the world. I had a deep sense of not being good enough, so I would strive to learn more facts, do more good, give more love, and achieve more goals. Despite being pursued by multiple suitors I couldn't seem to keep a relationship to save my life. My heart ached for love, the love and acceptance I didn't feel I deserved, but desperately wished for.

Many people are surprised to learn that I suffered from a lack of self-love and depression for decades. But it's true, I didn't love myself and I felt like a fraud.

My tactic to deal with the internal gloom was to achieve more success, attain more degrees and certifications, and accumulate more accolades for my work. I would give my time and money to family, friends, and charities — things that our culture says will make us happy and honorable. However, when I achieved something great I'd see only the faults, the imperfections; all the places where I had fallen short of my ideal. After all the work and sacrifice I didn't even allow myself to enjoy the fruits of my labor. I didn't enjoy the mental or emotional boost of a job well done. Instead, fearing that my ego would get puffed up, I denied the brilliance of my accomplishments. Even while others cheered, applauded, and congratulated me, I never felt good enough. I didn't feel worthy of admiration.

Part of this tendency came from my childhood. When my parents divorced I was three years old. I missed my father terribly and we lived in different states so I only saw him a couple of times each year. My father, who grew up in a poor family, believed that getting an education and a "stable job" were the most important goals to achieve. He emphasized to me again and again that the only worthy goal for me was to study, get good grades, and go to college. When I did well in school it got me praise and positive attention from him.

Though I knew my father loved me in between the times when report cards came out, the pursuit of knowledge and a pattern of seeking achievement for praise was firmly engrained in my mental makeup. Needless to say, a great deal of the accomplishments in my life were initiated by my insatiable need for approval, first from my father, later from my medical colleagues, and finally from the media. The drive to succeed and to accumulate degrees, certifications, and honorable mentions was what motivated me. It was never-ending, unfulfilling and totally exhausting!

I hid behind a protective shell of doing, but I was dying inside.

To make matters worse, I never felt like I was good enough. I was plagued by the dreaded "Imposter Syndrome." I was constantly anxious and worried that someone would discover I didn't really know my stuff, that I was a fraud. I didn't dare show how pitiful I felt because I had made that mistake before. I was met with looks of disbelief as those around me said I should be grateful for all that I had. I *was* grateful, but I didn't feel proud or fulfilled. My reputation for teaching and inspiring others left me isolated. I had no one to confess how I really felt. I hid behind a protective shell of doing, but I was dying inside.

Eventually, I realized that no matter how much I achieved, how much money I made, or how rich my personal lifestyle was it would always be society's ideal, not mine. So somewhere around age thirty, I began the several-year-long process of shedding my perfectionistic skin and to stop trying to live up to my father's ideal of accomplishment and success. I stopped doing things for the sake of looking good and relaxed my standards. I soon discovered that other things in life could bring me true joy and fulfillment. After years of therapy and soul-searching I learned that the depression I experienced wasn't solely linked to my insatiable childlike need for approval, nor was it purely biochemical. My sadness was also caused by my denial to fully express the desire of my soul to create and perform artistically.

To understand this better, let me take you back a few years in my timeline. Throughout my childhood I could be found on stage, on TV, or performing at my mother's house parties. This was the time when I felt most happy and fully alive. However, my father always told me that musicians and actors are a dime a dozen and that there were no guarantees that I could support myself as a performing artist. So as an adult I denied my soul its full creative expression. I held back the most passionate part of myself because I mistakenly believed that the arts were frivolous, and that being a healer would be more worthwhile. In my case, was I ever wrong!

Always curious and constantly researching my own journey of self-loathing, depression, and anxiety, led me to ask a lot of questions about life and love. While searching for relief from my own mental anguish I hit rock bottom and I cried out to the Divine for help. It was during a serious emotional low point in 2005, my "dark night of the soul." My life felt like a lie, except for that glorious night in the South of France. I was on a retreat-style vacation where, in true artist fashion, I courageously sang my heart out to a club of partygoers who didn't know my name or boring US TV image. It was pure bliss! And it was a far cry from the boring routine I lived back in the US, the very dim life I was set to return to in a matter of days.

Following the ecstasy of entertaining as my most bold self I returned to my hotel room in Cannes. All alone, the familiar dark mood returned when I realized that in just three days time I'd have to return to my life in America.

It was then that I cried out to God to take it all — my body, talents, and business. I sobbed, "I don't know what I'm doing with my life! YOU take it!"

I was wracked with an intense longing for meaning, a glimmer of joy, and some kind of relief. I wasn't suicidal, I would not have harmed myself. But I did want out of my personal pain. In total despair, I sobbed and flung myself onto the bed; my body trembled intensely. What happened next was a mystical, out of body, near-death-like experience where I thought God was answering my prayer to end my life.

My Near-Death-Like Experience and The End Of The Old Me

I felt as though I'd melted into the bed and an immense feeling of inner peace overtook me. Shaking, crying, and desperately praying for relief, I suddenly saw an all-consuming, intense white light. Confused, thinking the sun in Cannes couldn't possibly get any brighter, I squinted, trying to find the source of the light. To my surprise it was coming from *inside* me. I felt myself being drawn into the light as my body seemed to disappear.

I no longer felt like *me*. I was aware of the concept of *Andrea Pennington*, but I felt *more* than she. I felt complete Oneness and absolute, pure love. I felt love for myself and all of existence! It was the most beautiful feeling of calm and peace. My struggle to feel better seemed to finally come to a serene end. Though unseen, I sensed the presence of a non-physical loving being next to me. The awareness I gained caused an instantaneous shift in my entire existence.

From a detached perspective I saw an overview of my entire life, in an instant. As it flashed before me, I understood how each of my choices led me to my depressive state. No explanations were needed. I simply knew the source of my overwhelming sense of misery. It was comforting to be free from the pain of life.

Several important lessons were shown to me that totally set me free, which I now share with you (and anyone who will listen) to give you the keys to your own freedom. There are several insights which came with such clarity that they need to stand alone to be appreciated, so I will sprinkle them throughout the pages of this book. For now, these are a few realizations, or Truths, that bear knowing up front.

1. From that expanded state of awareness, I realized that in life on Earth, there is a Spirit, Source energy, Love or pure consciousness, which inhabits all things. And I saw and

experienced how I am one, united with that spirit or consciousness. In fact, no matter how separate we may feel at times, I saw that *we are all one* with that consciousness.

2. Though I am one with all consciousness I have my own spirit or higher self that is aware of every minute of my present and each of my past lifetimes. It also knows the cause of my present, past, and future troubles, and triumphs.

3. In addition to my spirit, I also have my own life essence — a soul. The human soul is an accumulation of past experiences, karma and genetic information passed down through time. Each soul has particular tendencies and preferences, which I call the "spiritual DNA."

4. My spirit is meant to be in control of my life as a human being. And as a co-creator of my life on earth, I am free to become what *I* choose — whether consciously or unconsciously. The earthly expression of my spiritual essence is totally of *my* choosing and that there is no "wrongness" in my choice. There is no God judging me, but my actions bear fruit and consequences. When I am ready, my spirit can even help me transcend or go beyond my past programming — both the programming I received during this lifetime, and even past lifetimes of soul programming and agreements.

5. As my true self is spirit and as an offshoot of pure consciousness, I am totally lovable, perfect, and complete. No matter the drama and trauma my soul has accumulated or endured—at our core we are all truly lovable.

During that out of body experience I realized that my whole life had been leading me to one major realization, something that our spirit knows all along: in order to enjoy a life of total wellness and happiness on earth we must become and express who we really are — not who our parents, society, or religion force us to be. None of our past programming, life experience, or trauma dictates, or limits who we are or who we can become.

The understanding of these principles was instantaneous and certain. I felt with complete assuredness that to live a life of freedom and joy, we can align our actions with our spirit, rather than the ego or programs of the soul. To do so we must learn who we really are, love who we are and live who we are. We are creators of life, including our own.

In that state of bliss, another stream of messages flowed to me and I was filled with a quiet joyful sense of well-being. Here are a few more of the messages which eased my emotional pain instantly. They are critical to you understanding the material in this book:

1. It's normal to want to be seen for who we are, that's why we came to play in this game of life on earth. We all want to be embraced and cherished for who we *really* are, that's our birthright. We all want to express ourselves wholeheartedly and to share ourselves meaningfully with others, that is our soul's greatest desire.

2. True happiness comes from within and it comes naturally when we integrate our whole being — mind, body, spirit, and soul.

3. We are all born with a deep desire to have an impact in the world, and to feel fulfilled knowing that we make a difference because deep down, our spirit reminds us that we DO matter.

4. You are a divine spiritual being with a perfect soul.

5. In this life you are meant to express your true feelings and desires.

6. You are meant to embody your soul's consciousness in your own chosen way in the precious human body you were given.

7. You are entitled to enjoy the unique talents, gifts, and body you've been given to thrive and to live life fully.

8. Because you were born this way, you are inherently perfect just as you are. Despite the errors you may have made, and the self-judgments and erroneous beliefs that hide your soul's light, the perfect, whole, lovable Light that you truly are still shines. No matter your looks, no matter your behavior, you are magnificent, just as you are!

I hope these messages give you comfort, as they did for me. I realized that I'm not wrong, bad, or selfish for wanting to feel like I matter and for wanting to be seen for who I really am.

As I allowed the peace of Oneness to bypass and replace all my previous thinking and biases, a vision of myself appeared in my awareness. I saw myself living joyfully on the French Riviera. In this vision of a new life I was with a child, I was singing professionally and I could heal people with my hands. Though stunned by the bizarreness of this life vision, I was inspired. In fact, I felt a total acceptance to return to my life, but with renewed enthusiasm to live according to my deepest desires. I said, "Yes" to Life and a few days later I returned to America a changed woman. There was no returning to the inauthentic version of me.

I am now committed to helping you achieve the same freedom, hopefully with less pain and drama!

With love,

Andrea Pennington, MD, C.Ac.

* This chapter is an excerpt from *I Love You, Me: My Journey to Overcoming Depression and Finding Real Self-Love* by Andrea Pennington, reprinted with permission.

Part 4
Manifesting & the Law of Attraction

It seems the time has arrived when science, mysticism and spirituality are agreeing on more points than a few. We are learning how our subconscious brains can help or hinder us from realizing our full potential. We are discovering the various ways our past traumas linger in the tissues of our bodies, including our brains, and how we can dispel those painful blemishes so that we can feel free to create new experiences. We even hear on so many TV shows that the secrets, lies and shameful past experiences we hide show up as limiting beliefs that rob us of our power to manifest what we *really* want in life.

How many life circumstances, in alignment with our deepest wishes and desires which just seem to show up as if by magic, showed up because we worked the law versus these things appearing because they were predestined for us? There are very few people who deny that synchronicity and coincidences happen more frequently the more we expect them to. The more we mindfully intend to see change in our lives the more the universe seems to line up with our intentions. For most people it is not a perfect science — yet.

All of these led me to ask whether *we* are consciously using the Law of Attraction to manifest these happenings, or if the Laws of the Universe are *using us*.

The concepts of karma, destiny and fate often come up when people talk about how we can manifest anything we want in life using the Law of Attraction. It's a sticky conversation to partake in, for sure.

Most people believe in the idea of 'free will' so they want to hold on to the hope that if we repeat our affirmations, create vision boards, and run mental movies long and hard enough, we can all be millionaires and celebrities with gorgeous spouses. But if our past deeds really do create the causes and conditions of our present and future reality, and if those past deeds were not creating sparkly clean karmic seeds, then all the wishing, hoping and visualizing won't do much — right?

I will not offer any definitive answer to this rather circuitous exploration, but I will say this: the universe is always bringing us the best possible outcome available to us. The seeds we have sown in the past — whether in this lifetime or past ones — determine the harvest we see in the now. But this should not deter us from deeply connecting to the feelings, images, sounds and scents of the future we wish to experience. Sometimes the journey to our intended destination will be filled with perilous twists and turns, but in the process, we may wind up settling our karmic accounts.

I'm inclined to believe that if we hold our precious visions in mind and surrender to the will of the divine we may just be delivered from our past wrongs with new insights and wisdom. Along our journey we are given the opportunity to live with more of the holy virtues of kindness, compassion, purity, honesty, integrity and love — generating positive karma, fortune or merit. By being in selfless service to others, and through meditation and contemplation, we can perform a type of *karma yoga* which can help us ease the pain and suffering of our karmic accounts so that we can realize more of our potential and see our dreams manifest into reality.

So with this I invite you to enjoy a few real life examples of how the power of belief and deep desire unlocked the magical power of manifesting with the Law of Attraction.

We Bought a Farm – But We're Not Farmers!

Charlotte Banff

The Winds of Change

Sometimes The Universe just takes over our life and shows us now it's time for the next adventure. The nudging of The Universe can come in many forms. Sometimes we're ready and sometimes we're reluctant to hear the call. Sometimes listening to that inner voice from The Divine, requires a level of understanding and readiness inside of us, that is not yet there. And that's where The Universe kicks in and if we're too reluctant, the nudging becomes just that; a kick!

After more than 20 years working a high-stress, high-performance job in the IT-industry, I've experienced my fair share of burnouts. I've literally hit the floor several times and every time I would get back up, dust myself off and get right back on the hamster wheel, trying to bend the laws of physics, pushing my body past what it was capable of.

I worked long hard hours, driven to be the best, bowing down to my need for success. The pressure was sending my body into a downward spiral, in a continuous vicious cycle of breaking down and getting back up. Although I was not yet conscious of how, the presence of my limitations to perform to my own high standards, brought up a deep need to shift my perception of how to live my life.

I have always known, that I was called to work with animals. When I'm with animals, my heart feels at home and my soul feels alive. With animals, I feel a creative power and a sense of connection to Spirit, something greater than myself or this physical world. I have come to learn through my work with animals, that they are far better at staying connected with this non-physical energy than we humans are. To the animals, that spiritual energy is all that is real.

When I allow myself to listen to and feel the spiritual energy of animals, I can see that they are operating purely from the heart, offering honesty without judgement. I have also discovered that I have a natural, effortless and ever present ability to "listen" to their messages, stories and feelings. Hearing them is easy too. I can hear them, very clearly. I hear their stories. I can feel what they are feeling. This Knowingness has just been there in me.

To me this connection feels completely natural and incorporated into my whole energy system. It's not something to turn on or off, it's just there.

And So The Conversation Begins

I have always been able to feel the energy of animals on a deep level. When I open to this exchange, a dialogue takes form between us. This tells me how the animals are feeling, what they have experienced, and how different events have affected their lives. Being so tuned into the animal world, I receive messages from the spiritual world around the animals. I am guided by the non-physical realm towards changes that might be made in the physical lives of the animals which would allow for their transformation and healing. I am able to "translate" these messages into words, and then make recommendations to their human companions as to how best to support the transformation needed in the lives of themselves and their animal companions.

When animals are given the opportunity to share their story, it heals them, the same as it does for people. We are actually not that different, which we realize when we open ourselves up to understand each other.

My Animal Teachers

I've had amazing animals come into my life to guide and help me develop my skills within the art and craft of learning to speak the spiritual language of the animals. I believe animals come into our lives at exactly the right moment for us to engage in mutual guidance and healing. I believe each meeting has been orchestrated by our spiritual self and in accordance with our spiritual guides, before we even arrive in this physical incarnation. It's never coincidental. Never!

We, both humans and animals alike, have made an agreement on a soul level, before we entered this life. We have agreed to join this incarnation together, to support each other, to grow and learn together. And what a beautiful gift it is, to have a loving animal companion by our side, as we go through this life.

Each animal that has come into my life over the years, has found their way to me with each of their particular personalities, needs, behaviours and ways of relating to me, in exact accordance with what we each need to express and grow from, supporting and helping each other along the way of this life together.

Over the many years of doing spiritual, healing and consciousness work with animals, I cannot count how many times I've heard my clients say 'well, I was really not supposed to have this dog/cat/horse …but they sort of just moved in and I'm so grateful that he/she did, because I've learned so so much'. In my opinion, they come in exactly the moment, that right moment when we need to receive their loving gifts the most.

Animals As Our Helpers

The gifts that animals have offered me and those I have worked with, are deeper insights into concepts such as togetherness, connectedness, kinship and love. But we can also learn a thing or two about what happens when we're not following our inner calling. Animals can truly orchestrate shifts in our life's journey towards better alignment with our souls purpose, when we are not where we are suppose to be in life. Over the years of doing this work, I've learned a lot from animals about what it means to be authentic, to speak my truth, stand my ground and to listen to my inner voice, but also what happens if I don't listen.

A few years ago, I had three horses boarded at three different stables and was doing a ridiculous amount of driving as a result. At home, our beloved dogs also needed my attention and care, and I constantly felt pulled in many directions. I was taking very good care of my animals, of course, but I constantly had that inner nagging voice that said that I wasn't doing enough for them. At the same time I was trying to balance my IT-career, including my own consulting business, and an animal healing business on top of that. The pressure and overload of it all began to affect my health. My schedule was always jam packed, running from one thing to the other. My life was like a house of cards just waiting to collapse. And then, it did.

I had broken down with stress before. Several times actually. I had always brushed it aside, gotten back up, dusted myself off to keep going. However, this time was different. Once again I found myself on the floor, but this time I couldn't get up. I was dizzy, my head was throbbing, my ears were ringing and my body just slammed on the brakes. No more!, it screamed. I finally knew that I could not go on like this. I'd pushed it too far this time. My body was demanding that something had to change.

My husband and I had been dreaming about owning a farm for many years. Hubby wished for space for construction projects and for his motorcycle, close enough to the fjords for kayaking. I wanted room for dogs, horses, and cats, and I dreamt about growing organic vegetables, too. It had to be within fair driving distance from Copenhagen, but also in the countryside, affordable, and spacious, but not too large. We wanted enough land to farm, to financially support the costs of owning a farm. Not too old, not too new. The list of requirements was insanely long. Our wishes were more or less impossible to fulfill on our budget and we had been searching unsuccessfully for the right place, for more than 10 years.

Magical Manifestation!

One day, 5 years ago, we were finishing off the very last bit of 15 years of renovations on our house. We had rented a lift to paint some woodwork on the roof. The paint was still wet on our roof, as we drove out to return the lift to the rental center. The rental center was located at a beautiful old farm not far away from our house. And here it was! Not only was it for sale, it was perfect! It fit perfectly with everything we had hoped and dreamed of.

We had always promised ourselves that we would never be those people who finished renovating an old house from A-Z, only to sell it the very next day. But now we are those people. Literally!

Once again, the Universe had set up in perfect synchronicity exactly what we needed. Through my spiritual work, I had gained trust of these types of synchronous signs. But this decision was bigger than anything we had ever done before. It felt so scary to want something so bad. There were so many pieces that had to fall into place before we could successfully call ourselves real farmers. We needed to sell our house, in order to afford the farm. Contract meetings were to be held with the bank and with our accountants. Meetings were scheduled with the agricultural services agency, in order to budget the business aspects of the farm. It was a complicated process, that could easily go on for a very very long time.

Despite all the challenges and all that which could go wrong in the process, we had a clear feeling that *this was it*. It was as if we could already *feel* how life would be living on this farm! It felt like a *knowing* inside, that this was where we belonged. We could feel it in our bones. Our bodies are spiritually connected and they are our vehicle of manifestation. When you *feel a vision in your body*, it's recognized on a spiritual level and that's when manifestation occurs. When we change our vibration, we change our life!

We *had* to live on that farm. *Period!* But how is that even possible for two IT-consultants, with no farming experience whatsoever, to run a farm, let alone a healing center? It was not the first time we have done this, my hubby and I. Starting a healing center together. We've done it before. Together. Several times in several lives.

How did we know this? We had previously, independently of each other, been seeking guidance from different mediums, who both told the same story: You two have been together before in previous lives! And we were told that in one life we created an Ashram together in India, and in another life, we founded a spiritual center in Greece, so maybe it was time to do it again, in this life? And yes, I believe in past lives. Yeah, I'm a nerdy healer!

We trusted this information because of just how right it felt in our bodies. This is what listening to the animals has given me, I learned to quiet myself and listen to what is conveyed to me from The Divine. I have been given access to so many levels of consciousness and in this quiet openness and connectedness, synchronicities are able to come into our lives and guide us. All we need to do is tune our energy system into the right frequency and we will be able to hear, exactly what we need to do next. All the guidance we need, is there for us, ripe for the picking.

Our dream was so real we could taste it, and yet it still felt so out of reach at the same time. All those years of dreaming about how life would be if we ever got a farm. We could almost feel all the wonderful day to day experiences awaiting us at the farm; being able to just grab a mug of tea and tiptoe into the stable in PJ's and say good morning to the horses, watching the stars over the fjords at night and following the seasons of farming the land and growing our own organic vegetables. Having dogs and horses together under one roof, no more driving around at all hours of the day!

This farm was the perfect place for us, with sufficient space for our healing workshops and spiritual retreats. With office facilities for our IT-consulting business and lots of space for my hubby's kayak and motorcycle! We had a beautiful sense of peace, like all the pieces of the puzzle of our life were finally falling into place.

It took only 3 months from the first day we saw the farm until we moved in.

Our house sold immediately. All the paperwork sailed right through. Meetings with the agricultural agency and all of the bank engagements went through effortlessly. It seemed like issues just solved themselves magically, in ways we could never have anticipated. It truly felt like someone had flicked a magic wand over the whole process and made it all happen. When The Universe snaps its fingers, magic truly happens!

The dream is now our reality, it has now been 5 years of hard farm work, aching muscles, and sore hands. Farm work has to be done in all kinds of weather, and at all hours, day or night. The farmer never sleeps. But every minute of it has been worth it.

The animals have continued to be amazing guides and helpers in my life, and it is my vision to share their spiritual voice as I hear it in my heart. I am committed to sharing this gift with others, as I truly believe that by listening to the profound wisdom from the Animal Kingdom, we can all learn a lot about life, spirituality and how to connect to the divine source within us. The animals have showed me how I can be authentic and in alignment with my soul. They have taught me how to listen to my inner voice, the voice that is always connected to Spirit and that never lies. It can be scary to listen to this bold truth as it may tell us things which are frightening to our sense of security and stability. But if we are courageous and dare to take a leap of faith, magic is just around that next corner.

With Love for Mother Nature and all her Animals,

Charlotte Banff

About the Author

Charlotte Banff is a Lightworker for The Animals.

Her vision is to share the spiritual voice of The Animals, globally.

Charlotte lives with her husband (and a lot of animals), on their farm in Denmark. They host a variety of spiritual activities on the farm, combining the connection to nature and animals in mindfulness retreats and events.

As an Animal Coaching Mentor, Charlotte guides people in spiritual growth, through Healing and Consciousness work with animals. She has founded *Animalhealer Academy*, an online program on interconnectedness between humans and animals, that broadens the knowledge of Animal Healing and Animal Communication.

She is an ambassador for two of the largest rescue centers for animals in Denmark. Her upcoming book *'The Animals Know'* addresses an alternative perspective on Animal Consciousness from a spiritual level and will broaden the knowledge of how to use and benefit from healing work for releasing trauma within Rescue Animals.

Connect with Charlotte online:
www.animalhealer.net
www.AnimalhealerAcademy.com
www.facebook.com/Animalhealer.netGlobal

You Are Great Beyond Belief

Trude Dybendahl

Hopelessness – January 1991

Who knew that feelings could be so overwhelming and paralyzing? I was convinced I could manage them all, but life has taken me to a place I have never been before. I'm scared. Scared that someone will find out and dig into that which I can't even handle myself. I feel like having walked to the end of a path, and from here I can't see anywhere to go.

The feeling of being in flow with laser clarity and tons of energy that I have had for so many months is gone. Choices were easy to make. I just knew what was right and had an enormous inner trust in both myself and the world. I have no idea where this force has gone, why it disappeared or how I can get it back again.

This was my state of being as I returned home from Russia where I had been doing a World Cup race in cross-country skiing. It didn't turn out well. I had to give up and quit the race after a few kilometres because of skis that were impossible to ski on. That was probably for the best. After all, my body didn't function well and my usual spark was gone. Something was wrong with me and I didn't know what.

A year and a half earlier I had decided I wanted to become a World Champion. Since that decision I had won several World Cup races and was well on my way towards my goal.

Bumps in the Road – December 1990

I was in Switzerland to make two more World Cup races before going home for the Christmas holidays. I had felt a little strange the last few days, with new thoughts and sensations of a kind I had never experienced before. I had a hunch that I should take a pregnancy test, but chose to postpone it until after the next upcoming World Cup races.

A few days later I was finally heading home for Christmas. The main focus for the upcoming three weeks would be to refresh my mental capacities and complete a period of excellent training before heading back to the World Cup races in January, which led up to the World Championships in February.

I was generally thrilled and so totally enjoyed my journey towards my big dream. The very next morning after coming home I took a pregnancy test. It was positive and my world stopped.

The Hiding

At that time, everything that involved having a baby was far into the future. I never had any doubts about what to do. Still, to have an abortion was a big and serious decision that created a multitude of mixed emotions.

I was a public figure in Norway, recognised almost everywhere I went. People frequently said hello and spoke to me in the streets, usually in a very kind way. Now I wanted to be invisible. I was anxious that the media would find out about it. The last thing

I needed was an article about my situation in one of the tabloid magazines. I couldn't stand the idea that strangers would know about this, which I was barely able to handle myself. I felt fragile and vulnerable, and that I needed to protect this very personal situation.

Only a few people were involved. My mother and father had always been very supportive, as they were during this time. In addition the national team coach, my ski club coach and the national team doctor were the only ones who knew.

The 24th of December, on Christmas Eve, my mother drove me to the hospital. I reflected on Jesus being born this day, and here I was about to do the opposite of giving birth. I certainly didn't feel good about what was to come.

After a day in the hospital I came home and went into a purely practical to-do mode. I tried to center myself and carefully return to my work: preparing for the world championship. I took it easier than originally planned, but otherwise had good workout days. It felt a bit weird not to talk to my close friends about my situation, but at the same time nice to just keep focused on the training.

On the surface everything looked fine. On the inside, unknowingly, an earthquake was building up. It didn't become clear until I travelled to Russia in the beginning of January for the next World Cup race, where I didn't make it to the finish line.

I returned home devastated, feeling lost and without a clue of what to do to get myself out of the confusion, internal mess and loss of personal power that I experienced.

I sought refuge in the night, to sleep off the despair, the heaviness and the paralysis I was feeling. It was six weeks until the World Championship, and I was miles away from performing on a champion level. I had to find a way out of this despair. My joy in life and my confidence were gone. Where do I go from here? I wondered before falling asleep.

The Vision

I kind of woke up at the crack of dawn, in the middle of a dream. Well, it was definitely not just another dream. It was more like a vision with a message. Being in the stage between sleeping and waking I was conscious that I was dreaming as the vision played out. It was crystal clear as if I was experiencing everything that was happening.

I am standing in a room without any light. The walls are so close to me that I can't really move. It is completely silent and dark, like there is no life at all in here. I feel trapped and have nowhere to move. Right at the tip of my nose is a door. It is locked and there is no key to open it. It is devastating being here. Suddenly I hear a voice. It is friendly, soft and clear. It says *"You will receive help to open the door."*

I suddenly find myself in a slightly bigger room, with about half a meter around me on each side. It's a bit lighter here, but quiet and kind of oppressive. I stand in front of a door with no handle and feel stuck to the ground. How on earth can this door be opened? I wonder. Just as I have had this thought I hear the voice again, calm, soft, and comforting. *"You will have to open this door with your mental power. You will have to want to do it."*

All of a sudden, the door opens and I stand in a doorway, almost blinded by the shining white light that is beaming towards me from the outside. I am looking out on a beautiful terrain covered with snow that sparkles like diamonds in the sun. There are no trees, just this huge open landscape, like farmland. The sparkling diamond snow dazzles me. I have never seen anything so beautiful. In a second, the heaviness within me is totally gone.

That's when I see him, just to the right of the doorway I'm standing in. I instinctively know it is his voice I have heard while being in the two closed, dark rooms. He is welcoming me with a big smile and his eyes are glowing of playfulness and pure kindness. It looks like he has been waiting for me the whole time. He reaches out his arms to welcome me out into this world of joy and glittering, white light. I hear him say in my mind, "Here you go, play! Enjoy! It is all yours to do". "Really?" I ask. The answer is a deep and fervent "Yes!"

Suddenly I'm on my cross-country skis, sitting in a downhill position the whole time while speeding both up hills and down hills! It is all happening without me striving, pushing or putting any effort into it. It happens with an ease and total sensation of flow. I am smiling, laughing, and cheering inside, being filled with an indescribable feeling of euphoria.

Memorizing

I just knew the vision had a message for me, so I went through it again and again, recalling every detail. With these scenes sharply etched into my memory, I woke up fully and the hopelessness of my reality washed over me again. I pondered, what on earth does this vision mean? And who was that person I saw? *"You will be helped to open the first door,"* he had said. Okay, but what kind of door, and what kind of help?

Just as these thoughts tumbled around in my head, the phone rang. I got out of bed and picked it up. It was my ski club coach, Erik. "How are you?" he asked and sounded tense. I had never heard him sound like this before. The strong "I can cope with everything" version of me answered: "I have felt better, but I'm okay". "I have been so scared", he continued. "I should never have let you go to Russia to compete in that World Cup race. It was too soon after the abortion."

That's when I realised he thought I had quit the race because of physical complications. Erik didn't know that I had quit the race because of my skis being impossible to ski on, not because of my health. He kept on talking: "I have been so worried that something was wrong, and I have broken the promise I gave you about not telling anyone." A wave of fear rushed over me; did anyone know? He continued, "I so sorry, but I just couldn't keep this to myself anymore. I had to talk to Nina." Nina is one of my good skiing friends. "She immediately saw that this is a really challenging situation for you," Erik continued. "You can call her any time of the day if you need someone to talk to."

I fell silent. *You will be helped to open the first door,* the voice had said. Right there and then I knew Nina would be the one to help me out of the first dark, room of emptiness, absent of joy, hope or faith. I thanked Erik and assured him that breaking his promise was indeed a good thing. I hung up and walked slowly back to the bed and collapsed onto it. A sense of relief spread through my body as I realized I didn't have to carry this burden alone anymore. Initially, I had thought this situation was something I could handle dispassionately. How wrong I was. I would finally face my suppressed emotions, my despair and mental chaos; the emotions I thought I could ignore by focusing my energy on tasks and activities.

I went back to my dream and replayed the next scene, standing in front of the second door. *"You will have to open this door with your mental power. You have to want to do it!"* It suddenly made so much more sense to me. I saw it was not about something I had *to do* to open the door. It was about my mental mindset. Did I want to go forward with trust and faith in me still being able to become the World Champion? Or would I stay in the past, dwelling in the pain? Did I still really want to win and do the work it demanded of me? Did I want to stay focused and look ahead? I faced my wants and needs, and reconsidered my decision from a year and a half ago. The answer was an unconditional yes.

My friend Nina became the pipeline out of the room of despair. I finally got to share my repressed feelings of fear and shame, thus allowing the necessary clearing of lower energy frequencies to air out of my field and space. The place of hopelessness that had been created by them had blocked my heart, created anxiety and hindered my joy and faith to flourish. With this space cleared I was ably to re-access my heart's joy, and regained my mental focus and determination.

The Vision Comes True – 12 February 1991

An intense feeling of calmness, excitement, and joy sparks me out of sleep early this morning. The day I have been preparing for during many years, and specifically in the last two years, is finally here. I will be on the starting line of the five kilometre race in just a few hours. The last weeks have been filled with different challenges all the way to the World Championships and my vision has been with me every day.

I know that today, more than ever, the present is the place to be. Not dwelling in the past or jumping into the future with questions like "what if I win today, or what if I fail?" I am connected to the joy, excitement and gratitude for being exactly where I want to be and doing what I so deeply love: skiing in nature, focused, prepared and performing.

Nobody skied faster than me that day. I won the gold medal, which added to the silver medal I won a few days before.

Understanding and Gratitude

I say with certainty that I wouldn't have won the gold medal without the vision six weeks earlier. It brought me out of a dead end into the emotions of euphoria, joy and playfulness which filled every cell of my body. I had been shown a possible future and it was my task to manifest it into physical reality.

Years later I realized that I had met one of my spiritual guides in the vision. The term "spiritual guide" was unfamiliar to me at the time. I just had this deep inner knowing that the vision *carried the truth*. I was guided out of the illusion of separation and strife, and back to the source of endless possibilities of co-creation, to the land of faith and trust – in my self, in my dreams and in my capacity to make magic real.

Dear reader, please know that everything is energy and energy is made of the frequencies of vibrations. If you want to create something amazing that is not a part of your reality today, you must raise your own energy frequency to match your desired future. At the time of my vision I didn't know this. But my guide did, and he facilitated the vision that programmed me for a future beyond my present reality. The emotions I experienced raised the energy-vibrations of my being to a totally different level. It matched the feelings of winning the gold medal. By this I was drawn towards that reality. But the choice was still mine to make. I was told I would have to really *want to* do it and do what I needed to do, which shows that mental force and action also have to be a part of creation.

Even if you haven't figured out your spiritual path, trust your inner knowing and the messages you receive from your heart; the channel of your soul and the spirit world. Whether guidance arrives in a dream state or by other forms of messaging; *listen, pay attention. Allow the Universe to help you and take action toward it.* This is what true co-creation is all about; creating a NEW physical reality together with the spirit realm, beyond the established thought patterns and habits residing in your brain.

Whether you are riding the waves of ease and joy or in the midst of a valley of darkness and doubt, your guides are always with you to show you your next steps and give you hope, faith and the guts to act. It is up to you to allow this co-creation to be a part of your life by setting your intentions for what you want to manifest, asking for help and then paying attention for guidance. Dare to make it a part of your daily life and you too will experience that life can be magical and even beyond your dreams.

About the Author

Trude Dybendahl helps people who want to transform their lives or need skills to be resilient in changing times. Her clients discover their magnificent potential and surpass limiting belief-systems that hold them in a state of strife, worry and inner stress. They experience a movement into faith, trust and conscious co-creation by learning the Conscious Self Leadership© method, CSLeadership, thus becoming their own, authentic changemaker.

Trude is a World Champion who won nine international medals in the Olympics and World Championships, in addition to eight World Cup victories. She has been a member of several boards and been involved in humanitarian projects through the Norwegian Red Cross, Olympic Aid, Amnesty International and the Norwegian Church Aid.

Trude is a transformational life coach, an Emotion Code practitioner, author and speaker She works with clients in Europe and USA and runs different personal development programs.

Connect with Trude Dybendahl:
www.TrudeDybendahl.no
Email post@trudedybendahl.no
www.facebook.com/TrudeDybendahl
www.instagram.com/trudedybendahl

Talking to Golden Arrow

Miriam Thiel-Alberts

I stood in front of the horse stall and looked at the regal, white horse. He was peacefully chewing the fresh hay, which scented the air in the old barn. I held out my hand for him to sniff and he blew his warm breath into it. His silky fur seemed to light the whole stable and his expression was curious. I heard the low chewing sounds of the other horses and I was slowly getting cold. It was January in Denmark and the winter had been long, grey, and miserable.

I leaned close and whispered, "Tomorrow you are mine Golden Arrow". The horse looked at me and nodded his head. The previous owner had called him "Indy", but his papers said Golden Arrow, so I was giving him a forever home and his beautiful name back. The owner didn't want to keep him as she couldn't train him. So she gave Golden Arrow to me for free. On my drive through the black night back to the Film School where I lived and worked, I thought about how this all had happened.

A year ago I had taken a job as head of film production at a college specialized in film making and moved from Germany to rural Denmark. The job and the move proved disappointing, the work atmosphere was hostile and frightening. Every time the principal yelled at me, I felt like I was seven years old again, standing between my fighting parents, hoping this time they wouldn't kill each other, while ducking from the things they threw at each other. We lived in a big house in an affluent neighbourhood and I desperately tried to hide the drama that occurred behind the closed doors of the pristine façade.

The day after a particularly loud and upsetting fight the night before, I went to my mother to cheer her up. I was happy, I knew what I wanted to be when I grew up: I wanted to be a princess, live in a castle with a handsome prince, and wear long pretty dresses. When I told my mother she sucked in the air noisily through her pursed lips and vehemently shook her head. "You will never be a princess as you were not born a princess!" Her curt and angry answer shook me and I felt ashamed for wanting such a foolish thing. The wish to become a princess went into a locked box in my heart and I never spoke of it again.

I grew up bitter and afraid of people learning my secret of wanting to feel like a princess. Mostly I had relationships with men who were not princes and certainly did not believe me to be their princess, and I felt I deserved this treatment. I had never felt really loved by my mother and because of it, I believed that if my mother couldn't love me, then I must not be worthy of love.

Most of my life I hated myself for my secret wish to be a princess. And now I was getting the white horse instead of the prince, I thought smiling. I went back to my spacious empty apartment and that night I dreamt about being a little girl again cantering on a white pony through the forest. I laughed as the trees flew past and I inhaled the aromatic cool air. The sun warmed my skin I felt so happy that I wanted this feeling to go on forever. Going to the horse stables and riding in the forest were my only joys when I was little. Those rare moments helped me survive the loveless environment I grew up in. When I was not with the ponies I protected my heart with thick, tall walls, afraid of getting hurt again, but even though they kept the pain away they also kept the love out.

Now, the little girl inside me had finally rebelled against my uncomfortable work situation and pushed me, after more than thirty years, to take up horseback riding again and to adopt a wild horse. I was not an experienced rider and Golden Arrow was definitely not a beginner's horse. He was also not interested in being trained, as his previous training attempts had made him feel very unsafe. Instead he had learned how to avoid uncomfortable situations by rearing, running away or simply bucking, which reminded me of my rebellion during my teenage years. But when the woman called and told me she wanted to give Golden Arrow to me for free, something inside me just said "yes". It was a "yes" to my inner child's dream to have my own horse, which I had locked away for a long time alongside my wish to be a princess.

I moved Golden Arrow to a stable close to me and visited him daily. He gave me an excuse to sneak away from the oppressive atmosphere at the college and his presence and big spirit calmed me. When it came to training he would allow it as long as I didn't ask him to do anything challenging. If I challenged him, he would fight against it.

A few weeks later I entered the principal's office for my end of year appraisal meeting and I knew immediately that something was wrong. I felt the hostile energy in the room and I wanted to run away. Although I was not expecting it at all, when the principal said, "We are not prolonging your contract" I just nodded silently. After that, the rest of the meeting was a blur and I left not really knowing what happened. I did however have the notion, that my contract was not prolonged, because I challenged the principal for proper elections for a worker's representative, in hope for a kinder and healthier work environment.

I went to Golden Arrow in a daze and cried hot tears into his long white mane. He stood still and breathed warm air into my neck. Somehow I knew things were going to be okay even though at that time I didn't know how. I needed to find a place for me and Golden Arrow and a job to support us quickly. But this time I decided not to worry about my dire situation and I applied for a training in Animal Communication and Healing. I felt this would help the bond between Golden Arrow and me and I had always intuitively connected with animals and knew how they felt.

I started my education close to Copenhagen a month after leaving my job. I concentrated on meditating daily and looking after myself. A couple of weeks before I had to leave the apartment at the college, out of the blue, I was offered a job at a horse livery stable. The job included a cosy apartment and I could bring my horse and cat.

I loved my apartment above the riding hall, overlooking the horse's fields. I looked after seventeen horses and had a lot of spare time to be with Golden Arrow. In the early morning when I went into the stable to feed the horses Golden Arrow would always greet me with a whinny. He would look at me with his smiling eyes as he happily followed me to the paddock to play with his new friends. In this peaceful, beautiful setting, I started to breathe again and the tension from the recent stress of my previous job slowly left my body.

Golden Arrow and I started training in the riding hall and he was now trying to follow my leads. There were still times when he got stressed and would just shut down or buck. But I would just go back and try it again. To help Golden Arrow in the training process I became a Reiki practitioner and gave him therapeutic healing on a regular basis, which he loved. I saw not only a big change in him, but also in me. I started experiencing profound happiness.

I always had the dream of cantering with my horse through the forest and I started riding with Golden Arrow in the forest, which was frightening for both of us at first. Golden Arrow was mostly attentive and happy, even though he would often get startled and afraid of things in the forest. Slowly I was starting to trust my feelings and my connection to Golden Arrow. When I felt he was getting overwhelmed I'd dismount and walk with him for a while. Trusting my feelings became a necessity to keep us both safe, as Golden Arrow could, in an instant, rear, buck and jump if he became too stressed. When we managed a trip through the forest we proudly came back to the farm feeling like championship winners.

After completing my animal communication training I wanted to talk to Golden Arrow. He was grazing in his paddock and when he saw me, he came over and looked at me curiously. The look in his eyes had changed so much over the past few months. His soft trusting gaze warmed my heart and I was curious what he would want to share with me. After a few moments, I saw him blinking his eye and in my mind I heard his message loud and clear, he told me, "I want to be in a film!" When I laughed he nodded his head a few times as if to tell me that I was right, then he turned around and trotted back to his hay. I stood there trying to understand what had just happened.

I had trained as a scriptwriter at university twelve years prior and since working at the horse farm I had only worked as a writer and editor sporadically. I liked the idea of writing another film with Golden Arrow as the star. I got to work immediately and prepared to film a short documentary about animal communication and healing during horse training. A friend of mine, a cameraman from Germany agreed to do the filming. The first morning as we put up the camera to catch the horses grazing calmly on the big summer field we were surprised to see that Golden Arrow was afraid of the camera. He would run away from it whenever we tried to film him. That's when it dawned on me that Arrow had not wanted to be in this film for himself.

Later we decided to set up the camera in front of his stall for an interview with me, so that Golden Arrow and I were in the same shot. When the cameraman turned on the equipment and nodded in my direction I took a deep breath and started telling our story. The words flowed not from me, but through me. I spoke for the very first time about me feeling abandoned and lonely as a child. As I spoke it became clear to me that I had projected these feelings onto Golden Arrow, as he had also been abandoned emotionally.

At the end of my speech, tears rolled down my face. I had not expected to get confronted by these old feelings. As I cried Golden Arrow caressed my face and I was filled with deep gratitude. I had spoken my truth. The silent little girl who had pretended that everything was fine had finally spoken up. I dried my face and we knew that this was going to be the heart of our short documentary. I realized I was finally feeling okay the way I was, and did not want to hide anything anymore.

When I am with Arrow I feel a deep bond between us and it is like we were meant for each other. After we finished the film I sat down and loudly exhaled. The rigid walls around my heart were slowly dissolving and I was starting to feel myself again.

When my film "Talking To Golden Arrow" was accepted into the prestigious film festival Equus in New York, I was filled with such joy and gratitude. In the hectic weeks before the festival I took Golden Arrow in from the field and he started bumping his head against my shoulder. I was annoyed at first but then suddenly thought of an old friend. We went to the same school, and met again several years later on Christmas Eve in our hometown. Our renewed friendship had unfortunately lasted only a few months, as I was off to film school and he moved from Germany to Los Angeles. Before he left he told me he had fallen in love with me, but I was unable to open my heart and made up an excuse about it not being the right time for me. I saw the sadness in his eyes and he never contacted me again. When I found out on social media that he had gotten married, my heart ached and I was sure we would never see each other again. I truly felt I had missed a big chance in my life. Years later I saw that he had taken down all the pictures from his wedding and a little glimpse of hope resurfaced.

A few days later as I cantered with Arrow through the beautiful forest, he suddenly stopped and looked back at me. I asked him what he wanted to tell me and I heard, "Invite him." I knew immediately who he meant and I was surprised, but I knew Golden Arrow was right. Back at the barn I sent my friend in Los Angeles a message to see if we wanted to join me in New York for the premiere of my film. To my surprise he responded yes. We agreed to meet at the cinema after not having seen each other for twelve years but when I saw him there leaning against the wall, my heart made a little jump.

During the screening of the film he was very touched by my film and I could see a little tear in his eye. Over the week of the premiere we became close friends again. I felt safe with him and we would talk and laugh for hours. This time felt different to all my other relationships because I was completely honest with him.

Six months later, when I visited him in Los Angeles, being together felt completely natural and we had the most wonderful time. On our last night we sat in bed, drinking a glass of champagne and eating strawberries. My heart was heavy with sadness knowing that I had to leave in the morning. It was late, the fan was humming and outside we could hear police sirens and heli-copters. He sat up and looked into my eyes and said, "I want to be together with you forever. Do you want to marry me?" I was somehow not shocked. I kissed him and said, "Yes". For the first time I really felt I belonged to somebody. I had come home emo-tionally. My horse had guided me to heal my heart, accept myself and finally find my true love.

Nearly on the day a year after we met in New York we were married in Denmark in a beautiful little church in the countryside. When I entered the church in my long white dress, the music started and I saw him waiting for me at the altar, I truly felt like a princess.

My deepest wish had came true because my horse asked me to be in a film and I finally could find the courage to open my heart for true love.

About the Author

Miriam Thiel-Alberts grew up in Germany, travelled the world as a stewardess and lived in the US, the UK, Italy, and Denmark. After hanging up her airline uniform she went off to film school, where she studied scriptwriting. She now works as a Writer, Animal Communicator and Healer, and Equine Coach. Miriam developed the Writing from the Heart with Horses method and her approach to teaching creative and biographical writing with her equine co-facilitators is unique. Her gentle and creative process with horses helps participants to connect with their subconscious stories in order to let go of old belief systems, move on from past trauma, and find their authentic voice.

Miriam's horse Golden Arrow who was the inspiration for her spiritual journey continuously guides her to explore the connection between the animal kingdom, Mother Earth, and humans.

She now lives outside of Berlin in the countryside with her husband, three cats, and her horse Golden Arrow.

Connect with Miriam:
www.animalwisdom.net
Email: animalwisdom@mail.com
www.facebook.com/groups/909640362489201
www.instagram.com/animalwisdomstories

Life is a Magic Miracle

Lene Heiselberg Vang

July 31, 2018

It's morning. I'm sitting on our couch in our kitchen looking out of the French glass doors. I love to sit here. It's such a calm and peaceful place. I often sit here writing or just looking out at our lovely garden, which is often visited by deer, pheasants, birds, cats, and butterflies. Right now I'm the only one awake. The house is quiet and I can hear the sum of the silence, that I love so much. My body and mind are at peace. This is one of many things, that I love about our property. It is kind of "close to the sound of silence". I am reminded about the beautiful song Sound of Silence by Simon and Garfunkel. It's such a beautiful song. I love their music and their soft intense sound filled with compassion, love and presence. It gives me the same feeling as the silence does. The feeling of just being.

These last few years I've learned a lot about attracting what I want in life by trusting, allowing, and following my impulses and the flow of life. That's what I believe life is about. Relaxing, trusting, and following what comes to us with courage and joy. We need only take one step at the time and surrendering into the wonderful now, with all our heart and soul. What would happen if we just allowed ourselves to follow that natural flow and trusting our heartfelt impulses in every moment?

I've had a lot of amazing experiences by trusting and following signs and the magical flow of life. I want to share with you a love story about what happened, when my husband and I followed our trust, joy, and impulses.

Meeting Lars

One day in September 2014 I asked the universe, "what is my next step"? I got the answer: "Go find a boyfriend". I smiled and thought, "Ok, lets see what happens". And life went on. Some weeks later I met a sweet couple at my cousin's birthday who had just met on a dating site. I got a strong impulse to make a profile on the same site and look for the man of my dreams.

3 days after creating the profile, he showed up in there. I got very curious and I just knew that I had to meet that man. Lucky me, he said yes to meeting, and the following weekend I drove the long distance to his place in another part of Denmark. He had packed a bag for us to take to a lovely beach at a forest, where we spent some magic, intense hours walking and talking. He was so visionary, interesting and different and I was very attracted to him. And suddenly we stood on the beach with our arms around each other in a long deep warm hug. It felt so good and right. I was filled with love and gratitude.

This lovely date, turned out to be the beginning of a lovely adventure.

The House

It was the last weekend in January 2015. It was cold and snowy, and I was visiting Lars, whom I had spent as much time with as possible since we met in the autumn.

It was one of our weekends at his place without the children, which I appreciated so much. We had a lot of time to enjoy each other's company. I loved to watch him cook delicious meals for us, while I sat listening to the fire that warmed up the room. I was in love, and I was so grateful for this lovely man, who already meant so much to me.

After breakfast Sunday morning Lars packed a thermos of tea, some fruit and snacks, and we went for a long walk in the snowy landscape. I loved the feeling of walking together, holding his hand and feeling his calm peaceful power. It made me feel safe and secure, and it often brought tears to my eyes (it still does to-day, almost 4 years later). We both loved walking in nature and we had some very good talks while walking. This time was more serious than usual, because we were talking about moving in to-gether at his place, next summer.

It was a big step for me to consider to move from my hometown, where my parents and friends lived, to another part of Denmark, where Lars was the only person I knew. It would also mean, that I would have to leave my good job and my col-leagues with whom I had worked for many years. It was scary, but it felt right. And I also knew that it would be a huge change for my children who, at that time, were close to leaving home.

Lars' house was small and it would be a challenge to create a home where all of our kids would feel at home. But we believed and trusted that we would find a good solution. We both had some debt from earlier relationships and we still owned houses with our former spouses. So, money was tight for both of us.

While we were walking we got excited about the idea of living together and how our life would be in the future. We decided to enjoy our warm tea when we arrived at the stream. Going down the road to the stream, we saw a big old timber and brick house with a 'For Sale' sign out front. It seemed empty so we looked through the windows and saw how beautiful it was. Everything was light and refurbished with respect for the old, charming house. We went to the garden and saw that the stream was running peacefully through it.

We fell in love with the property immediately and talked about how perfect and amazing it could be to live there together. We wondered what the price could be on such an old beautiful house next to the forest with a stream running through the garden. We allowed ourselves to dream about it even though it might be very expensive.

Coming back to Lars' place, the first thing we did was to look it up on the internet, but we couldn't find it anywhere. Our first thought was that it was sold. It was getting late and I had to go home, but Lars decided to search more and found out that the house would go up for auction in 10 days. This meant that it probably could be bought for much less money than its actual value.

All of this happened very fast and we went from talking about moving in together over six months to buying a house together within a few days. I knew it would mean a big change in my life, so I asked the universe for signs, to be sure I was doing the right thing. One day while driving home from work I got a strong impulse to visit a secondhand shop. I went in and looked around, wondering what I was supposed to find.

When I was about to leave I saw a beautiful hand painted house number that said 27, the same number as the house we wanted to buy. I smiled, laughed and got goosebumps all over. I just knew that it was a clear sign. I bought the beautiful number and from that moment I went all in on the house. We went to the place as often as possible in this process and every time we brought some personal things and flowers to the place, to show the place and the universe that we already felt that the house was ours.

To buy the house, we needed to provide 20% of the money in a very short time. And because of our debt no bank would lend us the money. So, we wrote to the lawyer representing the sale of the house with an offer. We proposed that we would buy the house as soon as one of our other houses sold, and we would like to rent it until then. He didn't answer, so we decided that I should go to the auction, not knowing what would happen. We had read that I should bring 10,000 Danish kroner if I wanted to offer on the house. So, we both raised what we had on our credits to get the money. When we went to the top of our credit accounts, we had exactly 10,000 Danish kroner.

I got the day off from work and was very nervous and excited at the same time. I met the lawyer just before the auction began and asked him about our offer. He just said, "Let's see what happens", and then the auction started. Other interested people where there to, including one couple eager to bid. The only way to get the house was to offer more than the others, so I started bidding, having absolutely no idea about how we could raise the 20% of the offer during the next week. I had decided to stop at one amount, but when the other couple upped their bid I did too. My last bid was a little bit higher. Then I heard the words: "1-2-3, the house is sold to that lady". I couldn't believe it. I'd bought a house, and had no clue about how to raise the money for it.

I gave the court the 10.000 kroner and got a small handwritten receipt. I called Lars, who had been waiting anxiously all day at work, and said. "I just bought a house". He was excited because he wanted the place just as badly as I did.

I couldn't believe what I just did. I was usually quite reasonable.

Then I went to see our new house. As I stood there, tears running down my cheeks, I got a strong feeling that this was meant to be our home. It felt so good and right, deep inside regardless of not knowing how we'd pay for it.

After calming down a bit, I called the lawyer, who told me where we could find the house key, and that we could move in the same day, if we wanted. I couldn't believe it.

It was time for me to go home to my children, and tell them everything. The first thing my daughter said when she saw me was, "Wow mum, you look so alive". That was exactly how I felt. Lars moved into the house with his kids the same day. He wanted to bring as much trust and good energy to our new home as possible.

The next two weeks were very intense. We had to come up with a lot of money in a very short time, if we wanted to keep the house. Lars called a friend and asked him if he had a good idea about how we could raise the money. His friend liked our crazy story and said that he would call back the next day with an idea. He did and we were about to raise 2/5 of the money! It was a good start. And finally, we got a yes from a bank that liked the story and trusted us. That was a miracle. Everything fell into place even though all odds were against us.

Today we are out of old debt. Our children love the house and our lovely garden, and often people from our cozy little village meet here at the stream for coffee or a beer to relax and enjoy life. This is our own little paradise. And we got it because we followed our impulses and trusted the process.

The universe brings us signs all the time. We only have to be open to them. I always ask for signs, that I am open to see, hear or smell. Oftentimes I see rainbows when I'm about to make big decisions. And when I am calm and aligned I see butterflies and find four-leafed clovers everywhere, which to me signal that I'm on the right path. Many times a big beautiful rainbow has showed up with our beautiful house in the center of it. And very often a song comes to my mind which gives answers to the situation I'm in.

We are never alone. The universe is always here to support us and shine the light for us.

The universe is telling me that it is just waiting for all of us to open up to the joyful and playful dance of love and prosperity that we came here to experience.

I'm grateful for this possibility to share my story with you. I hope that my words brought hope and tools for your magical and miraculous future.

About the Author

My name is Lene Heiselberg Vang. I was born in the southern part of Denmark. Since 1999 I have been a teacher for children with different diagnoses. When I was around 30 years old I began to be more and more interested in the spiritual world, which has lead to a lot of reading and courses in this field. Today I'm working with young adults as a teacher and a mentor to help them find their next step in life.

My husband and I have a retreat and course venue where people can come and connect with nature and their hearts wisdom by staying in our beautiful Mongolian Yurts. We offer personal coaching sessions and classes to teach people how to connect with nature and feel peace inside.

I am so blessed with my beautiful family. I have two amazing grown children who are the most loving and wonderful beings. They are the biggest miracles in my life. My lovely husband also has two sweet wonderful children, who bring us so much love, fun and joy in our daily life.

My mission is to inspire and help people to connect with their true divine essence and live their life from that blissful state of being.

Connect with Lene Heiselberg Vang:
www.facebook.com/LeneHeiselbergVang
Email: BeHuman@outlook.dk or peaceandjoy@outlook.dk

Conclusion

The stories in this book have probably opened your eyes to new possibilities. They certain have done that for me. I hope that expanding your mind and being open to magic will become a way of life for you now.

As I prepare to celebrate my birthday in a few weeks I am reflecting on the past year and the magical people who've come into my world, many of them are the co-authors of this book. Together we have challenged ourselves, taken bold moves to express our authentic voice and made a commitment to explore our hidden potential. Being connected to a loving community of heart-centered, soul-inspired change makers can inspire us to expand and evolve.

Consider yourself now connected to this tribe. You are no longer alone.

Feel free to contact the brilliant, brave authors in this book. They are so heart-centered and precious, I know they will inspire you as they have me. Besides, being in the company of amazing people allows their special sauce to rub off on us, and if we let it, their magical qualities can also linger.

If our paths should cross, I hope you will open up to share stories about your own mystical, magical experiences. Or perhaps you'll do so in one of my upcoming books or a live event?

I sincerely wish you a magical unfolding on your journey. May your life be rich with many blessings.

Here's to your miraculous life,

Andrea and all of the authors of Magic & Miracles

About the Book's Creator

Dr. Andrea Pennington is an integrative physician, acupuncturist, meditation teacher, and international speaker who is on a mission to raise the level of consciousness and love on our planet. As a personal brand architect, media producer, and communications specialist, she leverages her 20+ years of experience in broadcast and digital media to proudly help healers, Light workers and coaches to bring their brilliance to the world through publishing and media production with Make Your Mark Global Media.

Dr. Andrea is also a bestselling author, international TEDx speaker and documentary filmmaker. For nearly two decades, she has shared her empowering insights on vitality and resilience on the *Oprah Winfrey Show,* the *Dr. Oz Show,* iTV *This Morning,* CNN, the *Today Show,* LUXE-TV, Thrive Global and HuffingtonPost and as a news anchor for Discovery Health Channel. She also produced a four-part documentary series and DVD for Gaia entitled *Simple Steps to a Balanced Natural Pregnancy.*

Dr. Andrea has appeared in many print publications including *Essence, Ebony, Newsweek, The Sun, Red, Top Santé* and *Stylist.* She has also written or contributed to 10 books. As host of the talk show, *Liberate Your Authentic Self* and as founder of In8Vitality.com she blends her 'nerdy' mix of medical science, positive psychology, and mindfulness meditation to empower us all to show up authentically, love passionately, and live with vitality.

Visit Dr. Andrea online at:

www.AndreaPennington.com   www.RealSelf.Love
www.MakeYourMarkGlobal.com   www.In8Vitality.com

Get Social!
www.facebook.com/DrAndreaPennington
www.twitter.com/drandrea
www.linkedin.com/in/andreapennington
www.instagram.com/drandreapennington/

Other Books Published by Make Your Mark Global

Life After Trauma: Breaking the Silence to Inspire Resilience (My Life Rewritten Book 1) Compiled by Andrea Pennington

The Magical Unfolding: 8 Magical Processes for Peace, Potential and Purpose by Helen Rebello

The Ultimate Self-Help Book: How to Be Happy, Confident and Stress Free by Yvette Taylor

Finding Joy Beyond Childlessness by Lesley Pyne

I Love You, Me! My Journey to Overcoming Depression and Finding Real Self-Love Within by Andrea Pennington

The Orgasm Prescription for Women: 21 Days to Heightened Pleasure, Deeper Intimacy and Orgasmic Bliss by Andrea Pennington

The Book on Quantum Leaps for Leaders: The Practical Guide to Becoming a More Efficient and Effective Leader from the Inside Out by Bitta. R. Wiese

Turning Points: 11 Inspiring True Stories of Turning Life's Challenges into a Driving Force for Personal Transformation Compiled by Andrea Pennington

How to Liberate and Love Your Authentic Self by Andrea Pennington

The Top 10 Traits of Highly Resilient People by Andrea Pennington

Daily Compassion Meditation: 21 Guided Meditations, Quotes and Images to Inspire Love, Joy and Peace by Andrea Pennington

Eat to Live: Protect Your Body + Brain + Beauty with Food by Andrea Pennington